Schöningh

EinFach Englisch

Series Editor: Hans Kröger

Louis Sachar

Holes

Edited by
Wiltrud Frenken
Angela Luz
Brigitte Prischtt

Acknowledgements

Pictures

front and back cover: picture alliance/dpa; p. 4: © INTERFOTO/Mary Evans/ WALT DISNEY PICTURES/Ronald Grant Archive; pp. 41, 62: from Louis Sachar, *Holes*, Dell Laurel-Leaf, New York 1998, pp. 61, 99; p. 117: from Louis Sachar, *Holes*, Dell Laurel-Leaf, New York 1998, p. 193; p. 139: © picture-alliance/ Mary Evans Picture Library

Every effort has been made to supply complete copyright information for the texts and pictures included here. Should such entries be incomplete or contain errors, we request copyright owners to contact the publishers so that we can proceed with the necessary corrections.

Annotationen S. 140–144 und Idee zum Abschnitt "Developing skills", S. 145–148: Hans Kröger

Sprachliche Betreuung: Simone Duxbury-Ziemer

www.schoeningh-schulbuch.de
Schöningh Verlag, Jühenplatz 1–3, 33098 Paderborn

Druck A5 4 3 2 1 / Jahr 2019 18 17 16 15
Alle Drucke der Serie A sind parallel im Unterricht verwendbar.
Die letzte Zahl bezeichnet das Jahr dieses Druckes.

Umschlaggestaltung: Jennifer Kirchhof
Druck und Bindung: westermann druck GmbH, Braunschweig

ISBN 978-3-14-041276-6

Contents

Measurements used in the novel and their conversions

Measurement	**Conversion**
1 yard	0.9144 metres
1 foot	30.48 centimetres
1 inch	25.4 millimetres = 2.54 centimetres
1 pound	0.4536 kilogramme
degrees in Fahrenheit = [degrees in Celsius] x 1.8 + 32 e.g.: 80 degrees Fahrenheit = 26,6 degrees Celsius	degrees in Celsius = ([degrees in Fahrenheit] – 32) x $\frac{5}{9}$ e.g.: 0 degrees Celsius = 32 degrees Fahrenheit 100 degrees Celsius = 212 degrees Fahrenheit

Die mit einem ★ gekennzeichneten Vokabeln sind Teil des Lernwortschatzes.

Getting started

Breakfast is served at 4:30. (p. 14)

Madame Zeroni warned that if he failed to do this, he and his descendants would be doomed for all eternity. (p. 24)

There is no lake at Camp Green Lake. (p. 8)

"You're responsible for yourself. You messed up your life, and it's up to you to fix it." (p. 39, Mr. Pendanski)

She only kissed the men she killed. (p. 12)

The last thing he wanted to do after killing himself all day on the lake was to get in a fight with a boy called the Caveman. (p. 32)

Stanley told the truth, but perhaps it would have been better if he had lied a little. (p. 20)

1. Judging from the still and the quotes, what kind of novel do you expect *Holes* to be?
2. Speculate on the issues dealt with in *Holes*.

Acknowledgements

TO SHERRE, JESSICA, LORI, KATHLEEN, AND EMILY

AND TO JUDY ALLEN,
A FIFTH-GRADE TEACHER FROM WHOM WE
ALL CAN LEARN

PART ONE

YOU ARE ENTERING CAMP GREEN LAKE

1

There is no lake at Camp Green Lake. There once was a very large lake here, the largest lake in Texas. That was over a hundred years ago. Now it is just a dry, flat wasteland.

wasteland an area of land where nothing grows

There used to be a town of Green Lake as well. The town shriveled and dried up along with the lake, and the people who lived there.

degrees here: degrees Fahrenheit: a scale of temperature in which water freezes at 32° and boils at 212°; 95°F is equivalent to 35 °Celsius.

During the summer the daytime temperature hovers around ninety-five degrees in the shade – if you can find any shade. There's not much shade in a big dry lake.

ninety-five degrees 35° Celsius

The only trees are two old oaks on the eastern edge of the "lake." A hammock is stretched between the two trees, and a log cabin stands behind that.

The campers are forbidden to lie in the hammock. It belongs to the Warden. The Warden owns the shade.

warden here: the person in charge of a prison, who is responsible for making sure that its rules are obeyed

rattlesnake a poisonous American snake that shakes its tail to make a noise when it is angry; *Klapperschlange*

Out on the lake, rattlesnakes and scorpions find shade under rocks and in the holes dug by the campers.

Here's a good rule to remember about rattlesnakes and scorpions: If you don't bother them, they won't bother you.

Usually.

Being bitten by a scorpion or even a rattlesnake is not the worst thing that can happen to you. You won't die.

Usually.

Sometimes a camper will try to be bitten by a scorpion, or even a small rattlesnake. Then he will get to spend a day or two recovering in his tent, instead of having to dig a hole out on the lake.

lizard a type of reptile that has four legs and a long tail; *Eidechse*

But you don't want to be bitten by a yellow-spotted lizard. That's the worst thing that can happen to you.

You will die a slow and painful death.

Always.

If you get bitten by a yellow-spotted lizard, you might as well go into the shade of the oak trees and lie in the hammock. There is nothing anyone can do to you anymore.

hammock *Hängematte*

2

The reader is probably asking: Why would anyone go to Camp Green Lake?

Most campers weren't given a choice. Camp Green Lake is a camp for bad boys.

If you take a bad boy and make him dig a hole every day in the hot sun, it will turn him into a good boy.

That was what some people thought.

Stanley Yelnats was given a choice. The judge said, "You may go to jail, or you may go to Camp Green Lake."

Stanley was from a poor family. He had never been to camp before.

What kind of camp is Camp Green Lake? Find three adjectives to describe it.

jail a place where criminals are kept as part of their punishment; prison

3

Stanley Yelnats was the only passenger on the bus, not counting the driver or the guard. The guard sat next to the driver with his seat turned around facing Stanley. A rifle lay across his lap.

Stanley was sitting about ten rows back, handcuffed to his armrest. His backpack lay on the seat next to him. It contained his toothbrush, toothpaste, and a box of stationery his mother had given him. He'd promised to write to her at least once a week.

He looked out the window, although there wasn't much to see – mostly fields of hay and cotton. He was on a long bus ride to nowhere. The bus wasn't air-conditioned, and the hot, heavy air was almost as stifling as the handcuffs.

Stanley and his parents had tried to pretend that he was just going away to camp for a while, just like rich kids do. When Stanley was younger he used to play with stuffed animals, and pretend the animals were at camp. Camp Fun and Games he called it. Sometimes he'd have them play soccer with a marble. Other times they'd run an obstacle course, or go bungee jumping off a table, tied to broken rubber bands. Now Stanley tried to pretend he was going to Camp Fun and Games. Maybe he'd make some friends, he thought. At least he'd get to swim in the lake.

rifle a long gun which you hold up to your shoulder to shoot
to handcuff to put handcuffs *(Handschellen)* on sb
stationery paper for writing letters, usually with matching envelopes
stifling so hot and stuffy that it is difficult to breathe
★ **to pretend** to behave as if sth is true, even though you know it is not, in order to deceive people or for fun

camp Since summer school vacations in America are very long (usually two months), parents (who can afford it) often send their kids to summer camps where they are properly supervised and can play with kids their own age. There is a great variety of activities to choose from at these camps: sports, arts, science experiments, horse-riding, adventure games, etc.

obstacle course line of objects which people or animals have to jump over, climb through, etc., typically under time pressure or in a race

He didn't have any friends at home. He was overweight and the kids at his middle school often teased him about his size. Even his teachers sometimes made cruel comments without realizing it. On his last day of school, his math teacher, Mrs. Bell, taught ratios. As an example, she chose the heaviest kid in the class and the lightest kid in the class, and had them weigh themselves. Stanley weighed three times as much as the other boy. Mrs. Bell wrote the ratio on the board, 3:1, unaware of how much embarrassment she had caused both of them.

Stanley was arrested later that day.

He looked at the guard who sat slumped in his seat and wondered if he had fallen asleep. The guard was wearing sunglasses, so Stanley couldn't see his eyes.

Stanley was not a bad kid. He was innocent of the crime for which he was convicted. He'd just been in the wrong place at the wrong time.

It was all because of his no-good-dirty-rotten-pig-stealing-great-great-grandfather!

He smiled. It was a family joke. Whenever anything went wrong, they always blamed Stanley's no-good-dirty-rotten-pig-stealing-great-great-grandfather.

Supposedly, he had a great-great-grandfather who had stolen a pig from a one-legged Gypsy, and she put a curse on him and all his descendants. Stanley and his parents didn't believe in curses, of course, but whenever anything went wrong, it felt good to be able to blame someone.

Things went wrong a lot. They always seemed to be in the wrong place at the wrong time.

He looked out the window at the vast emptiness. He watched the rise and fall of a telephone wire. In his mind he could hear his father's gruff voice softly singing to him.

"If only, if only," the woodpecker sighs,
"The bark on the tree was just a little bit softer."
While the wolf waits below, hungry and lonely,
He cries to the moo–oo–oon,
"If only, if only."

It was a song his father used to sing to him. The melody was sweet and sad, but Stanley's favorite part was when his father would howl the word "moon."

The bus hit a small bump and the guard sat up, instantly alert.

middle school a school in the U.S. for children between the ages of 11 and 14

★ **to tease sb** to laugh and make jokes about sb to embarrass or upset them, sometimes in a friendly way, but often in an unkind way

ratio a relationship between two amounts, represented by a pair of numbers showing how much bigger one amount is than the other

unaware not noticing or realizing what is happening

★**innocent** here: not guilty of a crime
to be innocent of sth.
innocence the state of being not guilty of a crime

to convict sb of sth to officially find sb guilty of a crime

Gypsy *(pej.)* a member of a group of nomad people originally from India, who now live all over the world; also: Romany

★ **curse** a word or sentence used to ask God or a magical power to do sth bad to sb or sth; *Fluch*

descendant *Nachkomme*

woodpecker a bird that uses its long beak to make holes in trees; *Specht*

to howl to make a long, loud cry (like a wolf) because you are unhappy, angry, or in pain, or because you are amused or excited

alert giving all your attention to what is happening

Stanley's father was an inventor. To be a successful inventor you need three things: intelligence, perseverance and just a little bit of luck.

Stanley's father was smart and had a lot of perseverance. Once he started a project he would work on it for years, often going days without sleep. He just never had any luck.

Every time an experiment failed, Stanley could hear him cursing his dirty-rotten-pig-stealing-great-grand-father.

Stanley's father was also named Stanley Yelnats. Stanley's father's full name was Stanley Yelnats III. Our Stanley is Stanley Yelnats IV.

Everyone in his family had always liked the fact that "Stanley Yelnats" was spelled the same frontward and backward. So they kept naming their sons Stanley. Stanley was an only child, as was every other Stanley Yelnats before him.

All of them had something else in common. Despite their awful luck, they always remained hopeful. As Stanley's father liked to say, "I learn from failure."

But perhaps that was part of the curse as well. If Stanley and his father weren't always hopeful, then it wouldn't hurt so much every time their hopes were crushed.

"Not every Stanley Yelnats has been a failure," Stanley's mother often pointed out, whenever Stanley or his father became so discouraged that they actually started to believe in the curse. The first Stanley Yelnats, Stanley's great-grandfather, had made a fortune in the stock market. "He couldn't have been too unlucky."

At such times she neglected to mention the bad luck that befell the first Stanley Yelnats. He lost his entire fortune when he was moving from New York to California. His stagecoach was robbed by the outlaw Kissin' Kate Barlow.

If it weren't for that, Stanley's family would now be living in a mansion on a beach in California. Instead, they were crammed in a tiny apartment that smelled of burning rubber and foot odor.

If only, if only …

The apartment smelled the way it did because Stanley's father was trying to invent a way to recycle old sneakers. "The first person who finds a use for old sneakers," he said, "will be a very rich man."

It was this latest project that led to Stanley's arrest.

The bus ride became increasingly bumpy because the road was no longer paved.

Actually, Stanley had been impressed when he first found out that his great-grandfather was robbed by Kissin' Kate Barlow.

★**perseverance** determination to keep trying to achieve sth in spite of difficulties; *Beharrlichkeit*
to persevere to continue trying to do sth in a very determined way in spite of difficulties
persevering *beharrlich*

failure a lack of success in achieving or doing sth
stock market *Börse*
fortune a large amount of money; one's personal wealth

outlaw sb who has done sth illegal and is hiding from the law to avoid punishment, typically used for criminals in the past, esp. during the Wild West period in the USA (i.e. 2nd half of the 19th century). Famous outlaws of this time included Jesse James, Billy the Kid, Butch Cassidy, the Sundance Kid and Bonnie and Clyde.

mansion a large and expensive house
odor a smell, esp. an unpleasant one

arrest the act of capturing sb and taking them to a police station because it is believed that they have done sth illegal
to arrest sb for sth

Why is the road no longer paved?

to pave to cover a path, road, area, etc. with a hard, level surface, such as blocks of stone, asphalt or concrete

True, he would have preferred living on the beach in California, but it was still kind of cool to have someone in your family robbed by a famous outlaw.

Kate Barlow didn't actually kiss Stanley's great-grandfather. That would have been really cool, but she only kissed the men she killed. Instead, she robbed him and left him stranded in the middle of the desert.

"He was *lucky* to have survived," Stanley's mother was quick to point out.

The bus was slowing down. The guard grunted as he stretched his arms.

"Welcome to Camp Green Lake," said the driver.

Stanley looked out the dirty window. He couldn't see a lake. And hardly anything was green.

4

dazed unable to think clearly, esp. because of a shock or accident or tiredness

Stanley felt somewhat dazed as the guard unlocked his handcuffs and led him off the bus. He'd been on the bus for over eight hours.

"Be careful," the bus driver said as Stanley walked down the steps.

barren without plants

Stanley wasn't sure if the bus driver meant for him to be careful going down the steps, or if he was telling him to be careful at Camp Green Lake. "Thanks for the ride," he said. His mouth was dry and his throat hurt. He stepped onto the hard, dry dirt. There was a band of sweat around his wrist where the handcuff had been.

desolate empty and without people; very lonely and unhappy
desolation a state of ruin or destruction
desolated abandoned and totally without people

The land was barren and desolate. He could see a few rundown buildings and some tents. Farther away there was a cabin beneath two tall trees. Those two trees were the only plant life he could see. There weren't even weeds.

weed an unwanted plant growing wild

Juvenile Correctional Facility a kind of jail for young criminals that is designed to "correct" the error of their ways
violation an act that disregards a law, rule or promise
penal code a set of laws and the associated punishments for not obeying those laws

The guard led Stanley to a small building. A sign in front said, YOU ARE ENTERING CAMP GREEN LAKE JUVENILE CORRECTIONAL FACILITY. Next to it was another sign which declared that it was a violation of the Texas Penal Code to bring guns, explosives, weapons, drugs, or alcohol onto the premises.

As Stanley read the sign he couldn't help but think, *Well, duh!*

The guard led Stanley into the building, where he felt the welcome relief of air-conditioning.

A man was sitting with his feet up on a desk. He turned his head when Stanley and the guard entered, but otherwise didn't move. Even though he was inside, he wore sunglasses and a cowboy hat. He also held a can of soda, and the sight of it made Stanley even more aware of his own thirst.

He waited while the bus guard gave the man some papers to sign.

"That's a lot of sunflower seeds," the bus guard said.

Stanley noticed a burlap sack filled with sunflower seeds on the floor next to the desk.

"I quit smoking last month," said the man in the cowboy hat. He had a tattoo of a rattlesnake on his arm, and as he signed his name, the snake's rattle seemed to wiggle. "I used to smoke a pack a day. Now I eat a sack of these every week."

The guard laughed.

There must have been a small refrigerator behind his desk, because the man in the cowboy hat produced two more cans of soda. For a second Stanley hoped that one might be for him, but the man gave one to the guard and said the other was for the driver.

"Nine hours here, and now nine hours back," the guard grumbled. "What a day."

Stanley thought about the long, miserable bus ride and felt a little sorry for the guard and the bus driver.

The man in the cowboy hat spit sunflower seed shells into a wastepaper basket. Then he walked around the desk to Stanley. "My name is Mr. Sir," he said. "Whenever you speak to me you must call me by my name, is that clear?"

Stanley hesitated. "Uh, yes, Mr. Sir," he said, though he couldn't imagine that was really the man's name.

"You're not in the Girl Scouts anymore," Mr. Sir said.

Stanley had to remove his clothes in front of Mr. Sir, who made sure he wasn't hiding anything. He was then given two sets of clothes and a towel. Each set consisted of a long-sleeve orange jumpsuit, an orange T-shirt, and yellow socks. Stanley wasn't sure if the socks had been yellow originally.

He was also given white sneakers, an orange cap, and a canteen made of heavy plastic, which unfortunately was empty. The cap had a piece of cloth sewn on the back of it, for neck protection.

Stanley got dressed. The clothes smelled like soap.

★**to sign** to write your signature on a document to show that you wrote it, agree with it, or were present at an event
sunflower seed *Sonnenblumenkern*
burlap *Jute*
to quit to stop doing sth, esp. sth that is bad, unhealthy or annoying
to wiggle to move with small movements from side to side or up and down

Girl Scouts a well-known youth organization for girls, founded in the U.S. in 1912 by Juliette Low that seeks to develop certain skills for surviving in the outdoors, as well as important citizenship, and character values *(Pfadfinderinnenbewegung)*

What does Mr. Sir mean?

jumpsuit a one-piece item of clothing consisting of a shirt and a pair of trousers joined together
canteen a small, robust container in which water or other drinks are carried by soldiers, travelers, etc.

Mr. Sir told him he should wear one set to work in and one set for relaxation. Laundry was done every three days. On that day his work clothes would be washed. Then the other set would become his work clothes, and he would get clean clothes to wear while resting.

laundry dirty clothes that need washing

"You are to dig one hole each day, including Saturdays and Sundays. Each hole must be five feet deep, and five feet across in every direction. Your shovel is your measuring stick. Breakfast is served at 4:30."

foot a unit for measuring length, equal to 12 inches or about 30 centimeters. Five feet are equivalent to about 152 centimeters.

Stanley must have looked surprised, because Mr. Sir went on to explain that they started early to avoid the hottest part of the day. "No one is going to baby-sit you," he added. "The longer it takes you to dig, the longer you will be out in the sun. If you dig up anything interesting, you are to report it to me or any other counselor. When you finish, the rest of the day is yours."

★**counselor** sb whose job is to help and support people with questions or problems

Stanley nodded to show he understood.

"This isn't a Girl Scout camp," said Mr. Sir.

He checked Stanley's backpack and allowed him to keep it. Then he led Stanley outside into the blazing heat.

blazing extremely hot

"Take a good look around you," Mr. Sir said. "What do you see?"

Stanley looked out across the vast wasteland. The air seemed thick with heat and dirt. "Not much," he said, then hastily added, "Mr. Sir."

Mr. Sir laughed. "You see any guard towers?"

"No."

"How about an electric fence?"

★**fence** a structure made of wood, metal, etc. that surrounds a piece of land

"No, Mr. Sir."

"There's no fence at all, is there?"

"No, Mr. Sir.

"You want to run away?" Mr. Sir asked him.

Stanley looked back at him, unsure what he meant.

"If you want to run away, go ahead, start running. I'm not going to stop you."

Stanley didn't know what kind of game Mr. Sir was playing.

"I see you're looking at my gun. Don't worry. I'm not going to shoot you." He tapped his holster. "This is for yellow-spotted lizards. I wouldn't waste a bullet on you.

holster a leather holder for small gun that is worn on a belt

"I'm not going to run away," Stanley said.

"Good thinking," said Mr. Sir. "Nobody runs away from here. We don't need a fence. Know why? Because we've got the only water for a hundred miles. You want to run away? You'll be buzzard food in three days."

buzzard a type of large bird that eats dead animals

Stanley could see some kids dressed in orange and carrying shovels dragging themselves toward the tents.

"You thirsty?" asked Mr. Sir.

"Yes, Mr. Sir," Stanley said gratefully.

"Well, you better get used to it. You're going to be thirsty for the next eighteen months."

to drag oneself to move somewhere with difficulty, esp. because you are ill, tired, or unhappy
a drag 1. sth or sb that is boring; 2. sth that is annoying and continues for a long time
to be a drag on sb / sth to make it hard for sb to make progress towards what they want

5

What is Stanley thinking at that moment?

There were six large gray tents, and each one had a black letter on it: A, B, C, D, E, or F. The first five tents were for the campers. The counselors slept in F.

Stanley was assigned to D tent. Mr. Pendanski was his counselor.

"My name is easy to remember," said Mr. Pendanski as he shook hands with Stanley just outside the tent. "Three easy words: pen, dance, key."

Mr. Sir returned to the office.

Mr. Pendanski was younger than Mr. Sir, and not nearly as scary looking. The top of his head was shaved so close it was almost bald, but his face was covered in a thick curly black beard. His nose was badly sunburned.

"Mr. Sir isn't really so bad," said Mr. Pendanski. "He's just been in a bad mood ever since he quit smoking. The person you've got to worry about is the Warden. There's really only one rule at Camp Green Lake: Don't upset the Warden."

Stanley nodded, as if he understood.

"I want you to know, Stanley, that I respect you," Mr. Pendanski said. "I understand you've made some bad mistakes in your life. Otherwise you wouldn't be here. But everyone makes mistakes. You may have done some bad things, but that doesn't mean you're a bad kid."

Stanley nodded. It seemed pointless to try and tell his counselor that he was innocent. He figured that everyone probably said that. He didn't want Mr. Pen-dance-key to think he had a bad attitude.

"I'm going to help you turn your life around," said his counselor. "But you're going to have to help, too. Can I count on your help?"

"Yes, sir," Stanley said.

Mr. Pendanski said, "Good," and patted Stanley on the back.

***to upset sb** to make sb feel unhappy, angry or worried

pointless not likely to have any useful result

***attitude** the opinions and feelings that you usually have about sth

Two boys, each carrying a shovel, were coming across the compound. Mr. Pendanski called to them. "Rex! Alan! I want you to come say hello to Stanley. He's the newest member of our team."

weary very tired

The boys glanced wearily at Stanley.

They were dripping with sweat, and their faces were so dirty that it took Stanley a moment to notice that one kid was white and the other black.

barf bag *(slang) Kotzbeutel*

"What happened to Barf Bag?" asked the black kid.

"Lewis is still in the hospital," said Mr. Pendanski. He won't be returning." He told the boys to come shake Stanley's hand and introduce themselves, "like gentlemen."

"Hi," the white kid grunted.

"That's Alan," said Mr. Pendanski.

squid *zehnarmiger Tintenfisch*

X-ray a radiation beam that can go through solid objects to show what is inside, often used for photographing the inside of the body

"My name's not Alan," the boy said. "It's Squid. And that's X-Ray"

"Hey," said X-Ray. He smiled and shook Stanley's hand. He wore glasses, but they were so dirty that Stanley wondered how he could see out of them.

Rec Hall Recreation Hall: a place for relaxing and free-time activities

Mr. Pendanski told Alan to go to the Rec Hall and bring the other boys to meet Stanley. Then he led him inside the tent.

cot a camp bed

two feet about 61 centimeters

There were seven cots, each one less than two feet from the one next to it.

"Which was Lewis's cot?" Mr. Pendanski asked.

"Barf Bag slept here," said X-Ray, kicking at one of the beds.

"All right, Stanley, that'll be yours," said Mr. Pendanski.

Stanley looked at the cot and nodded. He wasn't particularly thrilled about sleeping in the same cot that had been used by somebody named Barf Bag.

crate a large carry box made of wood or plastic

Seven crates were stacked in two piles at one side of the tent. The open end of the crates faced outward. Stanley put his backpack, change of clothes, and towel in what used to be Barf Bag's crate. It was at the bottom of the stack that had three in it.

Squid returned with four other boys. The first three were introduced by Mr. Pendanski as José, Theodore, and Ricky. They called themselves Magnet, Armpit, and Zigzag.

armpit the hollow place under your arm where it joins your body

nickname a name used instead of a person's real name

"They all have nicknames," explained Mr. Pendanski. "However, I prefer to use the names their parents gave them – the names that *society will recognize them by* when they return to become useful and hardworking members of society."

"It ain't just a nickname," X-Ray told Mr. Pendanski. He tapped the rim of his glasses. "I can see inside you, Mom. You've got a big fat heart."

The last boy either didn't have a real name or else he didn't have a nickname. Both Mr. Pendanski and X-Ray called him Zero.

"You know why his name's Zero?" asked Mr. Pendanski. "Because there's nothing inside his head." He smiled and playfully shook Zero's shoulder.

Zero said nothing.

"And that's Mom!" a boy said.

Mr. Pendanski smiled at him. "If it makes you feel better to call me Mom, Theodore, go ahead and call me Mom." He turned to Stanley. "If you have questions, Theodore will help you. You got that, Theodore. I'm depending on you."

Theodore spit a thin line of saliva between his teeth, causing some of the other boys to complain about the need to keep their "home" sanitary.

"You were all new here once," said Mr. Pendanski, "and you all know what it feels like. I'm counting on every one of you to help Stanley."

Stanley looked at the ground.

Mr. Pendanski left the tent, and soon the other boys began to file out as well, taking their towels and change of clothes with them. Stanley was relieved to be left alone, but he was so thirsty he felt as if he would die if he didn't get something to drink soon.

"Hey, uh, Theodore," he said, going after him. "Do you know where I can fill my canteen?"

Theodore whirled and grabbed Stanley by his collar. "My name's not Thee-o-dore," he said. "It's Armpit." He threw Stanley to the ground.

Stanley stared up at him, terrified.

"There's a water spigot on the wall of the shower stall."

"Thanks ... Armpit," said Stanley.

As he watched the boy turn and walk away, he couldn't for the life of him figure out why anyone would want to be called Armpit.

In a way, it made him feel a little better about having to sleep in a cot that had been used by somebody named Barf Bag. Maybe it was a term of respect.

saliva the liquid that is produced naturally in your mouth, spit
sanitary clean and not causing any danger to people's health

relief a feeling of happiness when sth frightening, worrying, uncomfortable or painful ends or does not happen at all
***relieved** feeling happy because you are no longer worried about sth

collar the part of a shirt, coat, etc. that fits around your neck, and is usually folded over

spigot a tap, esp. on the outside of a building

not for the life of him *(colloq) beim besten Willen nicht*

term a word or expression that has a special meaning within a particular domain, esp. for a specific subject or type of language

6

Stanley took a shower – if you could call it that, ate dinner – if you could call it that, and went to bed – if you could call his smelly and scratchy cot a bed.

*scratchy rough and irritating against your skin

scarcity a situation in which there is not enough of sth; lack

Because of the scarcity of water, each camper was only allowed a four-minute shower. It took Stanley nearly that long to get used to the cold water. There was no knob for hot water. He kept stepping into, then jumping back from, the spray, until the water shut off automatically. He never managed to use his bar of soap, which was just as well, because he wouldn't have had time to rinse off the suds.

How long do you shower?

suds the mass of bubbles formed on the top of water with soap in it

stewed cooked slowly in liquid for a long time, esp. meat and vegetables

Dinner was some kind of stewed meat and vegetables. The meat was brown and the vegetables had once been green. Everything tasted pretty much the same. He ate it all, and used his slice of white bread to mop up the juice. Stanley had never been one to leave food on his plate, no matter how it tasted.

"What'd you do?" one of the campers asked him.

At first Stanley didn't know what he meant.

"They sent you here for a reason."

"Oh," he realized. "I stole a pair of sneakers."

The other boys thought that was funny. Stanley wasn't sure why. Maybe because their crimes were a lot worse than stealing shoes.

"From a store, or were they on someone's feet?" asked Squid.

"Uh, neither," Stanley answered. "They belonged to Clyde Livingston."

Nobody believed him.

"Sweet Feet?" said X-Ray. "Yeah, *right*!"

"No way," said Squid.

Now, as Stanley lay on his cot, he thought it was kind of funny in a way. Nobody had believed him when he said he was innocent. Now, when he said he stole them, nobody believed him either.

stolen base a special move in baseball

triple a hit of the ball in baseball that allows the batter to get to the third base

Clyde "Sweet Feet" Livingston was a famous baseball player. He'd led the American League in stolen bases over the last three years. He was also the only player in history to ever hit four triples in one game.

courtroom *Gerichtssaal*

Stanley had a poster of him hanging on the wall of his bedroom. He used to have the poster anyway. He didn't know where it was now. It had been taken by the police and was used as evidence of his guilt in the courtroom.

Clyde Livingston also came to court. In spite of everything, when Stanley found out that Sweet Feet was going to be there, he was actually excited about the prospect of meeting his hero.

Clyde Livingston testified that they were his sneakers and that he had donated them to help raise money for the homeless shelter. He said he couldn't imagine what kind of horrible person would steal from homeless children.

That was the worst part for Stanley. His hero thought he was a no-good-dirty-rotten thief.

As Stanley tried to turn over on his cot, he was afraid it was going to collapse under all his weight. He barely fit in it. When he finally managed to roll over on his stomach, the smell was so bad that he had to turn over again and try sleeping on his back. The cot smelled like sour milk.

Though it was night, the air was still very warm. Armpit was snoring two cots away.

Back at school, a bully named Derrick Dunne used to torment Stanley. The teachers never took Stanley's complaints seriously, because Derrick was so much smaller than Stanley. Some teachers even seemed to find it amusing that a little kid like Derrick could pick on someone as big as Stanley.

On the day Stanley was arrested, Derrick had taken Stanley's notebook and, after a long game of come-and-get-it, finally dropped it in the toilet in the boys' restroom. By the time Stanley retrieved it, he had missed his bus and had to walk home.

It was while he was walking home, carrying his wet notebook, with the prospect of having to copy the ruined pages, that the sneakers fell from the sky.

"I was walking home and the sneakers fell from the sky," he had told the judge. "One hit me on the head."

It had hurt, too.

They hadn't exactly fallen from the sky. He had just walked out from under a freeway overpass when the shoe hit him on the head.

Stanley took it as some kind of sign. His father had been trying to figure out a way to recycle old sneakers, and suddenly a pair of sneakers fell on top of him, seemingly out of nowhere, like a gift from God.

Naturally, be had no way of knowing they belonged to Clyde Livingston. In fact, the shoes were anything but sweet. Whoever had worn them had had a bad case of foot odor.

prospect the possibility that something will happen

to testify to make an official statement or give evidence in a court case

★**homeless shelter** a place where people who have no home can live for free

➔ Why does Stanley use these words to describe his hero's thoughts?

★**to donate** to give sth, esp. money, to a person or an organization in order to help them

donation sth, esp. money, that you give to a person or an organization in order to help them

★**to snore** to breathe in a noisy way through your mouth and nose while you are asleep

to torment to deliberately treat sb cruelly by continually annoying or hurting them

complaint an expression of dissatisfaction

★**to pick on sb** to bully sb; *drangsalieren*

to retrieve to find sth and bring it back

freeway overpass a bridge over a motorway

Stanley couldn't help but think that there was something special about the shoes, that they would somehow provide the key to his father's invention. It was too much of a coincidence to be a mere accident. Stanley had felt like he was holding destiny's shoes.

He ran. Thinking back now, he wasn't sure why he ran. Maybe he was in a hurry to bring the shoes to his father, or maybe he was trying to run away from his miserable and humiliating day at school.

A patrol car pulled alongside him. A policeman asked him why he was running. Then he took the shoes and made a call on his radio. Shortly thereafter, Stanley was arrested.

It turned out the sneakers had been stolen from a display at the homeless shelter. That evening rich people were going to come to the shelter and pay a hundred dollars to eat the food that the poor people ate every day for free. Clyde Livingston, who had once lived at the shelter when he was younger, was going to speak and sign autographs. His shoes would be auctioned and it was expected that they would sell for over five thousand dollars. All the money would go to help the homeless.

Because of the baseball schedule, Stanley's trial was delayed several months. His parents couldn't afford a lawyer. "You don't need a lawyer," his mother had said. "Just tell the truth."

Stanley told the truth, but perhaps it would have been better if he had lied a little. He could have said he found the shoes in the street. No one believed they fell from the sky.

It wasn't destiny, he realized. It was his no-good-dirty-rotten-pig-stealing-great-great-grandfather!

The judge called Stanley's crime despicable. "The shoes were valued at over five thousand dollars. It was money that would provide food and shelter for the homeless. And you stole that from them, just so you could have a souvenir."

The judge said that there was an opening at Camp Green Lake, and he suggested that the discipline of the camp might improve Stanley's character. It was either that or jail. Stanley's parents asked if they could have some time to find out more about Camp Green Lake, but the judge advised them to make a quick decision. "Vacancies don't last long at Camp Green Lake."

coincidence when two things happen at the same time, in the same place, or to the same people in a way that seems surprising or unusual
★destiny the things that will happen to sb in the future, esp. those that cannot be changed or controlled; fate
humiliating causing shame and embarrassment

to auction to sell sth at an auction (a public meeting where things are sold to the person who offers the most money for them)
★schedule here: a timetable of events
trial a legal process in which a judge, and often also a jury, examine information to decide whether sb is guilty of a crime or not
to delay to wait until a later time to do sth
★to afford to have enough money to buy or pay for sth
lawyer sb whose job is to advise people about laws, write formal agreements, or represent people in court
despicable extremely bad, immoral, or cruel

★to improve sth to make sth better
improvement the act of improving sth or the state of being improved

Why do Stanley's parents want to know more about Camp Green Lake? What does it tell you about their relationship?

vacancy a place that is not being used and is therefore free for sb else

7

The shovel felt heavy in Stanley's soft, fleshy hands. He tried to jam it into the earth, but the blade banged against the ground and bounced off without making a dent. The vibrations ran up the shaft of the shovel and into Stanley's wrists, making his bones rattle.

It was still dark. The only light came from the moon and the stars, more stars than Stanley had ever seen before. It seemed he had only just gotten to sleep when Mr. Pendanski came in and woke everyone up.

blade the flat cutting part of a sword, knife, shovel, etc.

to bounce off to hit and then move away from a surface; *abprallen*

dent a small hole or dip in the surface of sth usually caused by sth hitting it

Using all his might, he brought the shovel back down onto the dry lake bed. The force stung his hands but made no impression on the earth. He wondered if he had a defective shovel. He glanced at Zero, about fifteen feet away, who scooped out a shovelful of dirt and dumped it on a pile that was already almost foot tall.

might here: strength

to sting, stung, stung here: to cause sudden, sharp pain

defective not working properly

For breakfast they'd been served some kind of lukewarm cereal. The best part was the orange juice. They each got a pint carton. The cereal actually didn't taste too bad, but it had smelled just like his cot.

pint a unit for measuring an amount of liquid, esp. beer or milk. In Britain, a pint is equal to 0.568 litres, and in the U.S., it is equal to 0.473 litres.

Then they filled their canteens, got their shovels, and were marched out across the lake. Each group was assigned a different area.

to assign to give sb a particular job or make them responsible for sb or sth

The shovels were kept in a shed near the showers. They all looked the same to Stanley, although X-Ray had his own special shovel, which no one else was allowed to use. X-Ray claimed it was shorter than the others, but if it was, it was only by a fraction of an inch.

a fraction of an inch a very small amount

The shovels were five feet long, from the tip of the steel blade to the end of the wooden shaft. Stanley's hole would have to be as deep as his shovel, and he'd have to be able to lay the shovel flat across the bottom in any direction. That was why X-Ray wanted the shortest shovel.

The lake was so full of holes and mounds that it reminded Stanley of pictures he'd seen of the moon. "If you find anything interesting or unusual," Mr. Pendanski had told him, "you should report it either to me or Mr. Sir when we come around with the water truck. If the Warden likes what you found, you'll get the rest of the day off."

mound a pile of earth or stones that looks like a small hill

"What are we supposed to be looking for?" Stanley asked him.

"You're not looking for anything. You're digging to build character. It's just if you find anything, the Warden would like to know about it."

He glanced helplessly at his shovel. It wasn't defective. *He* was defective.

He noticed a thin crack in the ground. He placed the point of his shovel on top of it, then jumped on the back of the blade with both feet.

The shovel sank a few inches into the packed earth.

He smiled. For once in his life it paid to be overweight.

He leaned on the shaft and pried up his first shovelful of dirt, then dumped it off to the side.

Only ten million more to go, he thought, then placed the shovel back in the crack and jumped on it again.

He unearthed several shovelfuls of dirt in this manner, before it occurred to him that he was dumping his dirt within the perimeter of his hole. He laid his shovel flat on the ground and marked where the edges of his hole would be. Five feet was awfully wide.

He moved the dirt he'd already dug up out past his mark. He took a drink from his canteen. Five feet would be awfully deep, too.

The digging got easier after a while. The ground was hardest at the surface, where the sun had baked a crust about eight inches deep. Beneath that, the earth was looser. But by the time Stanley broke past the crust, a blister had formed in the middle of his right thumb, and it hurt to hold the shovel.

Stanley's great-great-grandfather was named Elya Yelnats. He was born in Latvia. When he was fifteen years old he fell in love with Myra Menke.

(He didn't know he was Stanley's great-great-grandfather.)

Myra Menke was fourteen. She would turn fifteen in two months, at which time her father had decided she should be married.

Elya went to her father to ask for her hand, but so did Igor Barkov, the pig farmer. Igor was fifty-seven years old. He had a red nose and fat puffy cheeks.

"I will trade you my fattest pig for your daughter," Igor offered.

"And what have you got?" Myra's father asked Elya.

"A heart full of love," said Elya.

"I'd rather have a fat pig" said Myra's father.

Desperate, Elya went to see Madame Zeroni, an old Egyptian woman who lived on the edge of town. He had become

crack a very narrow space between two things or two parts of sth

to pay here: to be an advantage

to pry up to lift sth with difficulty using a lever

edge a line or border at which a surface ends

surface the top layer of an area of water or land

inch a unit for measuring length, equal to 2.54 centimeters. Eight inches are equivalent to about 20 centimeters.

blister a swelling on your skin containing clear liquid, typically caused by continuous rubbing or as the result of a burn

Latvia a country in northeast Europe on the Baltic Sea, between Estonia and Lithuania; *Lettland*

Egyptian a native of Egypt – a country in NE Africa on the Mediterranean and Red Sea.

friends with her, though she was quite a bit older than him. She was even older than Igor Barkov.

The other boys of his village liked to mud wrestle. Elya preferred visiting Madame Zeroni and listening to her many stories.

to mud wrestle to fight sb by holding them and pulling or pushing them in wet earth that has become soft and sticky; *Schlammringen*

Madame Zeroni had dark skin and a very wide mouth. When she looked at you, her eyes seemed to expand, and you felt like she was looking right through you.

"Elya, what's wrong?" she asked, before he even told her he was upset. She was sitting in a homemade wheelchair. She had no left foot. Her leg stopped at her ankle.

"I'm in love with Myra Menke," Elya confessed. "But Igor Barkov has offered to trade his fattest pig for her. I can't compete with that."

"Good," said Madame Zeroni. "You're too young to get married. You've got your whole life ahead of you."

"But I love Myra."

"Myra's head is as empty as a flowerpot."

"But she's beautiful."

"So is a flowerpot. Can she push a plow? Can she milk a goat? No, she is too delicate. Can she have an intelligent conversation? No, she is silly and foolish. Will she take care of you when you are sick? No, she is spoiled and will only want you to take care of her. So, she is beautiful. So what? Ptuui!"

plow a piece of heavy metal farm equipment used to turn over the earth so that seeds can be planted
spoiled here: *verwöhnt*

Madame Zeroni spat on the dirt.

She told Elya that he should go to America. "Like my son. That's where your future lies. Not with Myra Menke."

But Elya would hear none of that. He was fifteen, and all he could see was Myra's shallow beauty.

Madame Zeroni hated to see Elya so forlorn. Against her better judgment, she agreed to help him.

shallow here: not deep and lasting
forlorn lonely and unhappy

"It just so happens, my sow gave birth to a litter of piglets yesterday," she said. "There is one little runt whom she won't suckle. You may have him. He would die anyway.

piglet a baby pig
runt the smallest and least developed baby animal of a group born at the same time
to suckle to give a baby or young animal milk from the breast or udder

Madame Zeroni led Elya around the back of her house where she kept her pigs.

Elya took the tiny piglet, but he didn't see what good it would do him. It wasn't much bigger than a rat.

"He'll grow," Madame Zeroni assured him. "Do you see that mountain on the edge of the forest?"

"Yes," said Elya.

"On the top of the mountain there is a stream where the water runs uphill. You must carry the piglet every day to the top of the mountain and let it drink from the stream. As it drinks, you are to sing to him."

She taught Elya a special song to sing to the pig.

"On the day of Myra's fifteenth birthday, you should carry the pig up the mountain for the last time. Then take it directly to Myra's father. It will be fatter than any of Igor's pigs."

"If it is that big and fat," asked Elya, "how will I be able to carry it up the mountain?"

"The piglet is not too heavy for you now, is it?" asked Madame Zeroni.

"Of course not," said Elya.

"Do you think it will be too heavy for you tomorrow?"

"No."

"Every day you will carry the pig up the mountain. It will get a little bigger, but you will get a little stronger. After you give the pig to Myra's father, I want you to do one more thing for me."

"Anything," said Elya.

"I want you to carry me up the mountain. I want to drink from the stream, and I want you to sing the song to me."

Elya promised he would.

Madame Zeroni warned that if he failed to do this, he and his descendants would be doomed for all of eternity.

At the time, Elya thought nothing of the curse. He was just a fifteen-year-old kid, and "eternity" didn't seem much longer than a week from Tuesday. Besides, he liked Madame Zeroni and would be glad to carry her up the mountain. He would have done it right then and there, but he wasn't yet strong enough.

to fail to do sth to not do what is expected, needed, or wanted
to doom to ensure that sb or sth will fail, die, be destroyed, etc.

Do you believe in curses? ➔

★**eternity** forever; all of time without end
curse a word or sentence used to ask God or a magical power to do sth bad to sb or sth; *Fluch*

Stanley was still digging. His hole was about three feet deep, but only in the center. It sloped upward to the edges. The sun had only just come up over the horizon, but he already could feel its hot rays against his face.

As he reached down to pick up his canteen, he felt a sudden rush of dizziness and put his hands on his knees to steady himself. For a moment he was afraid he would throw up, but the moment passed. He drank the last drop of water from his canteen. He had blisters on every one of his fingers, and one in the center of each palm.

Everyone else's hole was a lot deeper than his. He couldn't actually see their holes but could tell by the size of their dirt piles.

He saw a cloud of dust moving across the wasteland and noticed that the other boys had stopped digging and were watching it, too. The dirt cloud moved closer, and he could see that it trailed behind a red pickup truck.

three feet about 90 centimeters
to slope to be higher at one end than the other

dizziness *Schwindel*
to throw up to bring food and/or drink back up from your stomach and out through your mouth and nose because you are ill, to vomit
palm the inside surface of your hand

The truck stopped near where they were digging, and the boys lined up behind it, X-Ray in front, Zero at the rear. Stanley got in line behind Zero.

Mr. Sir filled each of their canteens from a tank of water in the bed of the pickup. As he took Stanley's canteen from him, he said, "This isn't the Girl Scouts, is it?"

Stanley raised and lowered one shoulder.

Mr. Sir followed Stanley back to his hole to see how he was doing. "You better get with it," he said. "Or else you're going to be digging in the hottest part of the day." He popped some sunflower seeds into his mouth, deftly removed the shells with his teeth, and spat them into Stanley's hole.

deft skillful

Every day Elya carried the little piglet up the mountain and sang to it as it drank from the stream. As the pig grew fatter, Elya grew stronger.

On the day of Myra's fifteenth birthday, Elya's pig weighed over fifty stones. Madame Zeroni had told him to carry the pig up the mountain on that day as well, but Elya didn't want to present himself to Myra smelling like a pig.

stone a unit for measuring weight, equal to 14 pounds or 6.35 kilograms. Fifty stones are equivalent to about 317 kilograms.

Instead, he took a bath. It was his second bath in less than a week.

Then he led the pig to Myra's.

Igor Barkov was there with his pig as well.

"These are two of the finest pigs I've ever seen," Myra's father declared.

He was also impressed with Elya, who seemed to have grown bigger and stronger in the last two months. "I used to think you were a good-for-nothing book reader," he said. "But I see now you could be an excellent mud wrestler."

"May I marry your daughter?" Elya boldly asked.

***bold** brave; willing to take risks

"First, I must weigh the pigs."

Alas, poor Elya should have carried his pig up the mountain one last time. The two pigs weighed exactly the same.

Stanley's blisters had ripped open, and new blisters formed. He kept changing his grip on the shovel to try to avoid the pain. Finally, he removed his cap and held it between the shaft of his shovel and his raw hands. This helped, but digging was harder because the cap would slip and slide. The sun beat down on his unprotected head and neck.

grip here: the way you hold sth

Though he tried to convince himself otherwise, he'd been aware for a while that his piles of dirt were too close to his hole. The piles were outside his five-foot circle, but he could see he was going to run out of room. Still, he pretended otherwise and kept adding more dirt to the piles, piles that he would eventually have to move.

The problem was that when the dirt was in the ground, it was compacted. It expanded when it was excavated. The piles were a lot bigger than his hole was deep.

It was either now or later. Reluctantly, he climbed up out of his hole, and once again dug his shovel into his previously dug dirt.

to excavate to make a hole in the ground by digging up soil

***reluctant** slow and unwilling
reluctance unwillingness and slowness in doing sth

previously before now or before a particular time

Myra's father got down on his hands and knees and closely examined each pig, tail to snout.

"Those are two of the finest pigs I have ever seen," he said at last. "How am I to decide? I have only one daughter."

"Why not let Myra decide?" suggested Elya.

"That's preposterous!" exclaimed Igor, expelling saliva as he spoke.

"Myra is just an empty-headed girl," said her father. "How can she possibly decide, when I, her father, can't?"

"She knows how she feels in her heart," said Elya.

Myra's father rubbed his chin. Then he laughed and said, "Why not?" He slapped Elya on the back. "It doesn't matter to me. A pig is a pig."

He summoned his daughter.

Elya blushed when Myra entered the room. "Good afternoon, Myra," he said.

She looked at him. "You're Elya, right?" she asked.

"Myra," said her father. "Elya and Igor have each offered a pig for your hand in marriage. It doesn't matter to me. A pig is a pig. So I will let you make the choice. Whom do you wish to marry?"

Myra looked confused. "You want me to decide?"

"That's right, my blossom," said her father.

"Gee, I don't know," said Myra. "Which pig weighs more."

"They both weigh the same," said her father.

"Golly," said Myra, "I guess I choose Elya – No, Igor. No, Elya. No, Igor. Oh, I know! I'll think of a number between one and ten. I'll marry whoever guesses the closest number. Okay, I'm ready."

"Ten," guessed Igor.

Elya said nothing.

"Elya?" said Myra. "What number do you guess?"

Elya didn't pick a number. "Marry Igor," he muttered. "You can keep my pig as a wedding present."

preposterous completely unreasonable or silly

*** to blush** to become red in the face, usually because you are embarrassed or nervous

blossom a single flower or all of the flowers on a tree or bush; here: a term of endearment
gee interjection used to show that you are surprised or annoyed
golly interjection used to express surprise

to mutter to speak in a low voice under your breath, esp. because you are annoyed about sth

What do you think of Elya's reaction?

The next time the water truck came it was driven by Mr. Pendanski, who also brought sack lunches. Stanley sat with his back against a pile of dirt and ate. He had a baloney sandwich, potato chips, and a large chocolate-chip cookie.

"How you doin'?" asked Magnet.

"Not real good," said Stanley.

"Well, the first hole's the hardest," Magnet said.

Stanley took a long, deep breath. He couldn't afford to dawdle. He was way behind the others, and the sun just kept getting hotter. It wasn't even noon yet. But he didn't know if he had the strength to stand up.

He thought about quitting. He wondered what they would do to him. What could they do to him?

His clothes were soaked with sweat. In school he had learned that sweating was good for you. It was nature's way of keeping you cool. So why was he so hot?

Using his shovel for support, he managed to get to his feet.

"Where are we supposed to go to the bathroom?" he asked Magnet.

Magnet gestured with his arms to the great expanse around them. "Pick a hole, any hole," he said.

Stanley staggered across the lake, almost falling over a dirt pile.

Behind him he heard Magnet say, "But first make sure nothing's living in it."

sack lunch lunch in a bag
baloney a type of sausage
to dawdle to take a long time to do sth or get somewhere
★**to quit** here: to stop working on a task without finishing it
expanse a large continuous area, esp. land, sky or water

After leaving Myra's house, Elya wandered aimlessly through the town, until he found himself down by the wharf. He sat on the edge of a pier and stared down into the cold, black water. He could not understand how Myra had trouble deciding between him and Igor. He thought she loved him. Even if she didn't love him, couldn't she see what a foul person Igor was?

It was like Madame Zeroni had said. Her head was as empty as a flowerpot.

Some men were gathering on another dock, and he went to see what was going on. A sign read:

DECK HANDS WANTED
FREE PASSAGE TO AMERICA

He had no sailing experience, but the ship's captain signed him aboard. The captain could see that Elya was a man of great strength. Not everybody could carry a full-grown pig up the side of a mountain.

★**aimless** not having a clear purpose or goal
wharf a structure that is built out into the water so that boats can stop next to it
foul disagreeable; offensive
deck hand sb who does physical work on a ship
to sign sb aboard to give sb a job on a ship

It wasn't until the ship had cleared the harbor and was heading out across the Atlantic that he suddenly remembered his promise to carry Madame Zeroni up the mountain. He felt terrible.
He wasn't afraid of the curse. He thought that was a lot of nonsense. He felt bad because he knew Madame Zeroni had wanted to drink from the stream before she died.

★envious wanting sth that sb else has, jealous
to envy sb sth to wish that you had someone else's possessions, abilities, etc.
envy the feeling of wanting sth that sb else has

to measure to find out the size, length, or amount of sth
steep *steil*

Zero was the smallest kid in Group D, but he was the first one to finish digging.
"You're finished?" Stanley asked enviously.
Zero said nothing.
Stanley walked to Zero's hole and watched him measure with his shovel. The top of his hole was a perfect circle, and the sides were smooth and steep. Not one dirt clod more than necessary had been removed from the earth.
Zero pulled himself up to the surface. He didn't even smile. He looked down at his perfectly dug hole, spat in it, then turned and headed back to the camp compound.
"Zero's one weird dude," said Zigzag.
Stanley would have laughed, but he didn't have the strength.
Zigzag had to be the "weirdest dude" Stanley had ever seen. He had a long skinny neck, and a big round head with wild frizzy blond hair that stuck out in all directions. His head seemed to bob up and down on his neck, like it was on a spring.
Armpit was the second one to finish digging. He also spat into his hole before heading back to the camp compound.
One by one, Stanley watched each of the boys spit into his hole and return to the camp compound.
Stanley kept digging. His hole was almost up to his shoulders, although it was hard to tell exactly where ground level was because his dirt piles completely surrounded the hole.
The deeper he got, the harder it was to raise the dirt up and out of the hole. Once again, he realized, he was going to have to move the piles.
His cap was stained with blood from his hands. He felt like he was digging his own grave.

weird very strange and unusual, and difficult to understand or explain
dude *(infm)* guy, man
frizzy very tightly curled

grave the place in the ground where a dead body is buried

In America, Elya learned to speak English. He fell in love with a woman named Sarah Miller. She could push a plow, milk a goat, and, most important, think for herself. She and Elya often stayed up half the night talking and laughing together.
Their life was not easy. Elya worked hard, but bad luck seemed to follow him everywhere. He always seemed to be in the wrong place at the wrong time.

He remembered Madame Zeroni telling him that she had a son in America. Elya was forever looking for him. He'd walk up to complete strangers and ask if they knew someone named Zeroni, or had ever heard of anyone named Zeroni. No one did. Elya wasn't sure what he'd do if he ever found Madame Zeroni's son anyway. Carry him up a mountain and sing the pig lullaby to him?

After his barn was struck by lightning for the third time, he told Sarah about his broken promise to Madame Zeroni. "I'm worse than a pig thief," he said. "You should leave me and find someone who isn't cursed."

"I'm not leaving you," said Sarah. "But I want you to do one thing for me."

"Anything," said Elya.

Sarah smiled. "Sing me the pig lullaby."

He sang it for her.

Her eyes sparkled. "That's so pretty. What does it mean?"

Elya tried his best to translate it from Latvian into English, but it wasn't the same. "It rhymes in Latvian," he told her.

"I could tell," said Sarah.

A year later their child was born. Sarah named him Stanley because she noticed that "Stanley" was "Yelnats" spelled backward.

Sarah changed the words of the pig lullaby so that they rhymed, and every night she sang it to little Stanley.

"If only, if only," the woodpecker sighs,
"The bark on the tree was as soft as the skies."
While the wolf waits below, hungry and lonely,
Crying to the moo–oo–oon,
"If only, if only."

Stanley's hole was as deep as his shovel, but not quite wide enough on the bottom. He grimaced as he sliced off a chunk of dirt, then raised it up and flung it onto a pile.

He laid his shovel back down on the bottom of his hole and, to his surprise, it fit. He rotated it and only had to chip off a few chunks of dirt, here and there, before it could lie flat across his hole in every direction.

He heard the water truck approaching, and felt a strange sense of pride at being able to show Mr. Sir, or Mr. Pendanski, that he had dug his first hole.

He put his hands on the rim and tried to pull himself up.

He couldn't do it. His arms were too weak to lift his heavy body.

lullaby a slow, melodic song sung to children to make them go to sleep or calm them down
barn a large building for storing crops or keeping farm animals
★**lightning** a powerful flash of light in the sky caused by a natural discharge of electricity in the atmosphere

chunk a large, uneven piece of sth
to fling, flung, flung to throw sth using a lot of force
to rotate to turn

rim the outside edge

He used his legs to help, but he just didn't have any strength. He was trapped in his hole. It was almost funny, but he wasn't in the mood to laugh.

"Stanley!" he heard Mr. Pendanski call.

Using his shovel, he dug two footholds in the hole wall. He climbed out to see Mr. Pendanski walking over to him.

to faint to suddenly become unconscious for a short time, to pass out

"I was afraid you'd fainted," Mr. Pendanski said. You wouldn't have been the first.

"I'm finished," Stanley said, putting his blood-spotted cap back on his head.

"All right!" said Mr. Pendanski, raising his hand for a high five, but Stanley ignored it. He didn't have the strength.

Mr. Pendanski lowered his hand and looked down at Stanley's hole. "Well done," he said. "You want a ride back?"

Stanley shook his head. "I'll walk."

Mr. Pendanski climbed back into the truck without filling Stanley's canteen. Stanley waited for him to drive away, then took another look at his hole. He knew it was nothing to be proud of, but he felt proud nonetheless.

He sucked up his last bit of saliva and spat.

8

A lot of people don't believe in curses.

A lot of people don't believe in yellow-spotted lizards either, but if one bites you, it doesn't make a difference whether you believe in it or not.

odd different from what is normal or expected, esp. in a way that you disapprove of or cannot understand

six to ten inches about 15 to 24 centimeters

Actually, it is kind of odd that scientists named the lizard after its yellow spots. Each lizard has exactly eleven yellow spots, but the spots are hard to see on its yellow-green body. The lizard is from six to ten inches long and has big red eyes. In truth, its eyes are yellow, and it is the skin around the eyes which is red, but everyone always speaks of its red eyes. It also has black teeth and a milky white tongue.

Looking at one, you would have thought that it should have been named a "red-eyed" lizard, or a "black-toothed" lizard, or perhaps a "white-tongued" lizard.

If you've ever been close enough to see the yellow spots, you are probably dead.

predatory bird a bird that hunts and eats other animals, esp. smaller ones

The yellow-spotted lizards like to live in holes, which offer shade from the sun and protection from predatory birds. Up to twenty lizards may live in one hole. They have strong, powerful legs, and can leap out of very deep holes to attack their prey. They eat small animals, insects, certain cactus thorns, and the shells of sunflower seeds.

prey an animal that is hunted and eaten by another animal
thorn a sharp point that grows along the stem of a plant to protect it, esp. on roses and cacti

9

Stanley stood in the shower and let the cold water pour over his hot and sore body. It was four minutes of heaven. For the second day in a row he didn't use soap. He was too tired.

There was no roof over the shower building, and the walls were raised up six inches off the ground except in the corners. There was no drain in the floor. The water ran out under the walls and evaporated quickly in the sun.

He put on his clean set of orange clothes. He returned to his tent, put his dirty clothes in his crate, got out his pen and box of stationery, and headed to the rec room.

A sign on the door said WRECK ROOM.

Nearly everything in the room was broken; the TV, the pinball machine, the furniture. Even the people looked broken, with their worn-out bodies sprawled over the various chairs and sofas.

X-Ray and Armpit were playing pool. The surface of the table reminded Stanley of the surface of the lake. It was full of bumps and holes because so many people had carved their initials into the felt.

There was a hole in the far wall, and an electric fan had been placed in front of it. Cheap air-conditioning. At least the fan worked.

As Stanley made his way across the room, he tripped over an outstretched leg.

"Hey, watch it!" said an orange lump on a chair.

"You watch it," muttered Stanley, too tired to care.

"What'd you say?" the Lump demanded.

"Nothin'," said Stanley.

The Lump rose. He was almost as big as Stanley and a lot tougher. "You said something." He poked his fat finger in Stanley's neck. "What'd you say?"

A crowd quickly formed around them.

"Be cool," said X-Ray. He put his hand on Stanley's shoulder. "You don't want to mess with the Caveman," he warned.

sore hurting; in pain
six inches about 15 centimeters
drain the hole in the bottom of a bath or sink that water flows out through
to evaporate *verdampfen*
rec room a place for recreational (free-time) activities
wreck the remains of sth that has been severely damaged or broken
pinball *Flipper*
to sprawl to lie or sit with your arms or legs stretched out in a lazy or careless way
pool a game similar to billiards that is often played in bars
bump a small raised area on a surface
to carve to form by cutting with a knife
★**initials** the first letters of all of your names in order
felt a thick soft material; *Filz*
fan here: a machine with turning blades which cool the air in a room by moving it around
lump an undefined, irregularly-shaped mass of sth solid
to demand here: to ask forcefully
to mess with to get involved with sb or sth that may cause problems or be dangerous

"The Caveman's cool," said Armpit.

"I'm not looking for trouble," Stanley said. "I'm just tired, that's all."

The Lump grunted.

X-Ray and Armpit led Stanley over to a couch. Squid slid over to make room as Stanley sat down.

"Did you see the Caveman back there?" X-Ray asked.

"The Caveman's one tough dude," said Squid, and he lightly punched Stanley's arm.

vinyl upholstery a type of strong plastic material covering an armchair or sofa

Stanley leaned back against the torn vinyl upholstery. Despite his shower, his body still radiated heat. "I wasn't trying to start anything," he said.

***to come to sb's rescue** to save sb who is in a dangerous situation
rescue when sb or sth is rescued from danger
rescue operation

The last thing he wanted to do after killing himself all day on the lake was to get in a fight with a boy called the Caveman. He was glad X-Ray and Armpit had come to his rescue.

"Well, how'd you like your first hole?" asked Squid.

to groan to make a long, deep sound because you are in pain, upset, or disappointed

Stanley groaned, and the other boys laughed.

"Well, the first hole's the hardest," said Stanley.

"No way," said X-Ray. "The second hole's a lot harder. You're hurting before you even get started. If you think you're sore now, just wait and see how you feel tomorrow morning, right?"

"That's right," said Squid.

"Plus, the fun's gone," said X-Ray.

"The fun?" asked Stanley.

"Don't lie to me," said X-Ray. "I bet you always wanted to dig a big hole, right? Am I right?"

Stanley had never really thought about it before, but he knew better than to tell X-Ray he wasn't right.

"Every kid in the world wants to dig a great big hole," said X-Ray. "To China, right?"

"Right," said Stanley.

"See what I mean," said X-Ray. "That's what I'm saying. But now the fun's gone. And you still got to do it again, and again, and again."

"Camp Fun and Games," said Stanley.

"What's in the box?" asked Squid.

Stanley had forgotten he had brought it. "Uh, paper. I was going to write a letter to my mother."

"Your mother?" laughed Squid.

"She'll worry if I don't."

to scowl to look at sb in an angry or disapproving way

Squid scowled.

to wreck to ruin, destroy

Stanley looked around the room. This was the one place in camp where the boys could enjoy themselves, and what'd they do? They wrecked it. The glass on the TV was smashed, as if someone had put his foot through it. Every table and chair seemed to be missing at least one leg. Everything leaned.

to lean, leant, leant to bend over to one side

He waited to write the letter until after Squid had gotten up and joined the game of pool.

Dear Mom,

Today was my first day at camp, and I've already made some friends. We've been out on the lake all day, so I'm pretty tired. Once I pass the swimming test, I'll get to learn how to water-ski. I

He stopped writing as he became aware that somebody was reading over his shoulder. He turned to see Zero, standing behind the couch.

"I don't want her to worry about me," he explained.

Zero said nothing. He just stared at the letter with a serious, almost angry look on his face.

Stanley slipped it back into the stationery box.

"Did the shoes have red X's on the back?" Zero asked him.

It took Stanley a moment, but then he realized Zero was asking about Clyde Livingston's shoes.

"Yes, they did," he said. He wondered how Zero knew that. Brand X was a popular brand of sneakers. Maybe Clyde Livingston made a commercial for them.

Zero stared at him for a moment, with the same intensity with which he had been staring at the letter.

Stanley poked his finger through a hole in the vinyl couch and pulled out some of the stuffing. He wasn't aware of what he was doing.

stuffing soft material that is used to fill sth, such as a sofa or cushion

"C'mon, Caveman, dinner," said Armpit.

"You coming, Caveman?" said Squid.

Stanley looked around to see that Armpit and Squid were talking to him. "Uh, sure," he said. He put the piece of stationery back in the box, then got up and followed the boys out to the tables.

The Lump wasn't the Caveman. He was.

He shrugged his left shoulder. It was better than Barf Bag.

10

joint a part of your body that can bend because two bones meet there

***to ache** to hurt
ache 1. a continuous pain that is not sharp or very strong; 2. a strong, mostly unhappy, feeling

***waist** the narrow part in the middle of the human body between the ribs and the hips
***to replace** to take the place of

***miracle** an action or event, which is impossible according to the ordinary laws of nature, and is therefore thought to be caused by God
miraculous 1. very good, completely unexpected, and often very lucky; 2. a miraculous action or event, which is impossible according to the ordinary laws of nature and is therefore believed to be caused by God

***awesome** extremely impressive, serious, or difficult so that you feel great respect, worry, or fear

Stanley had no trouble falling asleep, but morning came much too quickly. Every muscle and joint in his body ached as he tried to get out of bed. He didn't think it was possible but his body hurt more than it had the day before. It wasn't just his arms and back, but his legs, ankles, and waist also hurt. The only thing that got him out of bed was knowing that every second he wasted meant he was one second closer to the rising of the sun. He hated the sun.

He could hardly lift his spoon during breakfast, and then he was out on the lake, his spoon replaced by a shovel. He found a crack in the ground, and began his second hole.

He stepped on the shovel blade, and pushed on the very back of the shaft with the base of his thumb. This hurt less than trying to hold the shaft with his blistered fingers.

As he dug, he was careful to dump the dirt far away from the hole. He needed to save the area around the hole for when his hole was much deeper.

He didn't know if he'd ever get that far. X-Ray was right. The second hole was the hardest. It would take a miracle.

As long as the sun wasn't out yet, he removed his cap and used it to help protect his hands. Once the sun rose, he would have to put it back on his head. His neck and forehead had been badly burned the day before.

He took it one shovelful at a time, and tried not to think of the awesome task that lay ahead of him. After an hour or so, his sore muscles seemed to loosen up a little bit.

He grunted as he tried to stick his shovel into the dirt. His cap slipped out from under his fingers, and the shovel fell free. He let it lie there.

He took a drink from his canteen. He guessed that the water truck should be coming soon, but he didn't finish all the water, just in case he was wrong. He'd learned to wait until he saw the truck before drinking the last drop.

The sun wasn't yet up, but its rays arced over the horizon and brought light to the sky.

He reached down to pick up his cap, and there next to it he saw a wide flat rock. As he put his cap on his head, he continued to look down at the rock.

He picked it up. He thought he could see the shape of a fish, fossilized in it.

He rubbed off some dirt, and the outline of the fish became clearer. The sun peeked over the horizon, and he could actually see tiny lines where every one of the fish's bones had been. He looked at the barren land all around him. True, everyone referred to this area as "the lake," but it was still hard to believe that this dry wasteland was once full of water.
Then he remembered what Mr. Sir and Mr. Pendanski had both said. If he dug up anything interesting, he should report it to one of them. If the Warden liked it, he would get the rest of the day off.
He looked back down at his fish. He'd found his miracle.

to peek here: to be only partially visible
barren without plants
to refer to here: to speak of, call
wasteland an area of land where nothing grows

He continued to dig, though very slowly, as he waited for the water truck. He didn't want to bring attention to his find, afraid that one of the other boys might try to take it from him. He tossed the rock, face down, beside his dirt pile, as if it had no special value. A short while later he saw the cloud of dirt heading across the lake.

*****value** importance, usefulness

The truck stopped and the boys lined up. They always lined up in the same order, Stanley realized, no matter who got there first. X-Ray was always at the front of the line. Then came Armpit, Squid, Zigzag, Magnet, and Zero.
Stanley got in line behind Zero. He was glad to be at the back, so no one would notice the fossil. His pants had very large pockets, but the rock still made a bulge.

bulge a curved mass on the surface of sth, usually caused by sth under or inside it

Mr. Pendanski filled each boy's canteen, until Stanley was the only one left.
"I found something," Stanley said, taking it out of his pocket.
Mr. Pendanski reached for Stanley's canteen, but Stanley handed him the rock instead.
"What's this?"
"It's a fossil," said Stanley. "See the fish?"
Mr. Pendanski looked at it again.
"See, you can even see all of its little bones," said Stanley.
"Interesting," said Mr. Pendanski. "Let me have your canteen."
Stanley handed it to him. Mr. Pendanski filled it, then returned it.
"So do I get the rest of the day off?"
"What for?"
"You know, you said if I found something interesting, the Warden would give me the day off."
Mr. Pendanski laughed as he gave the fossil back to Stanley. "Sorry, Stanley. The Warden isn't interested in fossils."
"Let me see that," said Magnet, taking the rock from Stanley.
Stanley continued to stare at Mr. Pendanski.

to dig *(slang)* to look at, take notice of sth

"Hey, Zig, dig this rock."

"Cool," said Zigzag.

Stanley saw his fossil being passed around.

"I don't see nothing," said X-Ray. He took off his glasses, wiped them on his dirty clothes, and put them back on.

"See, look at the little fishy," said Armpit.

11

Stanley returned to his hole. It wasn't fair. Mr. Pendanski had even said his fossil was interesting. He slammed his shovel into the ground and pried up another piece of earth.

After a while, he noticed X-Ray had come by and was watching him dig.

"Hey, Caveman, let me talk to you a second," X-Ray said.

Stanley put down his shovel and stepped up out of his hole.

"Say, listen," said X-Ray. "If you find something else, give it to me, okay?"

pig latin a constructed language game where words in English are changed according to a simple set of rules. Pig latin takes the first consonant (or consonant cluster) of an English word, moves it to the end of the word and suffixes an *'ay'* (for example, *pig* yields *igpay*, *banana* yields *ananabay*, and *trash* yields *ashtray*)

Stanley wasn't sure what to say. X-Ray was clearly the leader of the group, and Stanley didn't want to get on his bad side.

You're new here, right?" said X-Ray. "I've been here for almost a year. I've never found anything. You know, my eyesight's not so good. No one knows this, but you know why my name's X-Ray?"

Stanley shrugged one shoulder.

"It's pig latin for Rex. That's all. I'm too blind to find anything."

rex *(Latin)* king

Stanley tried to remember how pig latin worked.

"I mean," X-Ray went on, "why should you get a day off when you've only been here a couple of days? If anybody gets a day off, it should be me. That's only fair, right?"

Why does Stanley agree? ➔

"I guess," Stanley agreed.

X-Ray smiled. "You're a good guy, Caveman."

Stanley picked up his shovel.

The more he thought about it, the more he was glad that he agreed to let X-Ray have anything he might find. If he was going to survive at Camp Green Lake, it was far more important that X-Ray think he was a good guy than it was for him to get one day off. Besides, he didn't expect to find anything anyway. There probably wasn't anything "of interest" out

***to survive** to manage to stay alive despite difficult conditions, such as an accident, war, or illness
survival the state of managing to stay alive despite difficult conditions
survivor sb who manages to stay alive despite difficult conditions, such as an accident, war, or illness

there, and even if there was, he'd never been what you could call lucky.

He slammed his blade into the ground, then dumped out another shovelful of dirt. It was a little surprising, he thought, that X-Ray was the leader of the group, since he obviously wasn't the biggest or the toughest. In fact, except for Zero, X-Ray was the smallest. Armpit was the biggest. Zigzag may have been taller than Armpit, but that was only because of his neck. Yet Armpit, and all the others, seemed to be willing to do whatever X-Ray asked of them.

As Stanley dug up another shovelful of dirt, it occurred to him that Armpit wasn't the biggest. He, the Caveman, was bigger. He was glad they called him Caveman. It meant they accepted him as a member of the group. He would have been glad even if they'd called him Barf Bag.

It was really quite remarkable to him. At school, bullies like Derrick Dunne used to pick on him. Yet Derrick Dunne would be scared senseless by any of the boys here.

As he dug his hole, Stanley thought about what it would be like if Derrick Dunne had to fight Armpit or Squid. Derrick wouldn't stand a chance.

He imagined what it would be like if he became good friends with all of them, and then for some reason they all went with him to his school, and then Derrick Dunne tried to steal his notebook …

"Just what do you think you're doing?" asks Squid, as he slams his hands into Derrick Dunne's smug face.

"Caveman's our friend," says Armpit, grabbing him by the shirt collar.

Stanley played the scene over and over again in his mind, each time watching another boy from Group D beat up Derrick Dunne. It helped him dig his hole and ease his own suffering. Whatever pain he felt was being felt ten times worse by Derrick.

★**to pick on sb** to bully sb; *drangsalieren*

to be scared senseless to be so scared that you cannot react

smug showing too much satisfaction with your own cleverness or success

to ease to lessen the pain or discomfort of sth

12

Again, Stanley was the last one to finish digging. It was late afternoon when he dragged himself back to the compound. This time he would have accepted a ride on the truck if it was offered.

***to nod** to move your head up and down, typically to show agreement or understanding

to plop down to let your body drop heavily

When he got to the tent, he found Mr. Pendanski and the other boys sitting in a circle on the ground.

"Welcome, Stanley," said Mr. Pendanski.

"Hey, Caveman. You get your hole dug?" asked Magnet.

He managed to nod.

"You spit in it?" asked Squid.

He nodded again. "You're right," he said to X-Ray. "The second hole's the hardest."

X-Ray shook his head. "The third hole's the hardest," he said.

"Come join our circle," said Mr. Pendanski.

Stanley plopped down between Squid and Magnet. He needed to rest up before taking a shower.

"We've been discussing what we want to do with our lives," said Mr. Pendanski. "We're not going to be at Camp Green Lake forever. We need to prepare for the day we leave here and join the rest of society."

"Hey, that's great, Mom!" said Magnet. "They're going to finally let you out of here?"

The other boys laughed.

"Okay, José," said Mr. Pendanski. "What do you want to do with your life?"

"I don't know," said Magnet.

"You need to think about that," said Mr. Pendanski. "It's important to have goals. Otherwise you're going to end up right back in jail. What do you like to do?"

"I don't know," said Magnet.

"You must like something," said Mr. Pendanski.

"I like animals," said Magnet.

"Good," said Mr. Pendanski. "Does anyone know of any jobs that involve animals?"

"Veterinarian," said Armpit.

"That's right," said Mr. Pendanski.

"He could work in a zoo," said Zigzag.

"He belongs in the zoo," said Squid, then he and X-Ray laughed.

"How about you, Stanley? Any ideas for José?"

Stanley sighed. "Animal trainer," he said. "Like for the circus, or movies, or something like that."

"Any of those jobs sound good to you, José?" asked Mr. Pendanski.

"Yeah, I like what Caveman said. About training animals for movies. I think it would be fun to train monkeys."

X-Ray laughed.

"Don't laugh, Rex," said Mr. Pendanski. "We don't laugh at people's dreams. Someone is going to have to train monkeys for the movies."

"Who are you kidding, Mom?" asked X-Ray. "Magnet's never going to be a monkey trainer."

"You don't know that," said Mr. Pendanski. "I'm not saying it's going to be easy. Nothing in life is easy. But that's no reason to give up. You'll be surprised what you can accomplish if you set your mind to it. After all, you only have one life, so you should try to make the most of it."

Stanley tried to figure out what he'd say if Mr. Pendanski asked him what he wanted to do with his life. He used to think he wanted to work for the F.B.I., but this didn't seem the appropriate place to mention that.

"So far you've all done a pretty good job at messing up your lives," said Mr. Pendanski. "I know you think you're cool." He looked at Stanley. "So you're Caveman, now, huh? You like digging holes, Caveman?"

Stanley didn't know what to say.

"Well, let me tell you something, Caveman. You are here on account of one person. If it wasn't for that person, you wouldn't be here digging holes in the hot sun. You know who that person is?"

"My no-good-dirty-rotten-pig-stealing-great-great-grandfather."

The other boys howled with laughter.

Even Zero smiled.

It was the first time Stanley had ever seen Zero smile. He usually had such an angry expression on his face. Now he had such a huge smile it almost seemed too big for his face, like the smile on a jack-o'-lantern.

"No," said Mr. Pendanski. "That person is you, Stanley. You're the reason you are here. You're responsible for yourself. You messed up your life, and it's up to you to fix it. No one else is going to do it for you – for any of you."

Mr. Pendanski looked from one boy to another. "You're all special in your own way," he said. "You've all got something to offer. You have to think about what you want to do, then do it. Even you, Zero. You're not completely worthless."

The smile was now gone from Zero's face.

"What do you want to do with your life?" Mr. Pendanski asked him.

Zero's mouth was shut tight. As he glared at Mr. Pendanski, his dark eyes seemed to expand.

"What about it, Zero?" asked Mr. Pendanski. "What do you like to do?"

"I like to dig holes."

*__to kid__ to say sth that is not true, esp. as a joke
to accomplish to succeed in doing sth, esp. after trying very hard, to achieve
to set one's mind to sth to focus on a goal and think of nothing else

F.B.I. (Federal Bureau of Investigation) the police department in the U.S. that is controlled by the central government and that deals with crimes that break national laws rather than state laws

*__appropriate__ correct or suitable for a particular time, situation, or purpose
*__on account of__ because of

jack-o'-lantern a pumpkin with a face cut into it and a candle inside that is used as a decoration on Halloween
It's up to you to fix it. It is your responsibility to correct your mistake.

*__worthless__ here: without any good qualities or useful skills

to glare to look angrily at sb for a long time

↑ Find adjectives to describe the boys' attitudes towards their future.

13

All too soon Stanley was back out on the lake, sticking his shovel into the dirt. X-Ray was right: the third hole was the hardest. So was the fourth hole. And the fifth hole. And the sixth, and the ...

He dug his shovel into the dirt.

to lose track of sth to fail to remember or notice sth

After a while he'd lost track of the day of the week, and how many holes he'd dug. It all seemed like one big hole, and it would take a year and a half to dig it. He guessed he'd lost at least five pounds. He figured that in a year and a half he'd be either in great physical condition, or else dead.

pound a unit for measuring weight, equal to 16 ounces or 0.4536 kilograms. Five pounds are equivalent to about 2.2 kilograms

He dug his shovel into the dirt.

It couldn't always be this hot, he thought. Surely it got cooler in December. Maybe then they froze.

He dug his shovel into the dirt.

His skin had gotten tougher. It didn't hurt so much to hold the shovel.

As he drank from his canteen he looked up at the sky. A cloud had appeared earlier in the day. It was the first cloud he could remember seeing since coming to Camp Green Lake.

occasionally now and then

★to tease here: to make sb hopeful but not satisfy their wishes

to glisten to reflect light; to sparkle

He and the other boys had been watching it all day, hoping it would move in front of the sun. Occasionally it got close, but it was just teasing them.

His hole was waist deep. He dug his shovel into the dirt. As he dumped it out, he thought he saw something glisten as it fell onto the dirt pile. Whatever it was, it was quickly buried.

Stanley stared at the pile a moment, unsure if he'd even seen it. Even if it was something, what good would it do him? He'd promised to give anything he found to X-Ray. It didn't seem worth the effort to climb out of his hole to check it out.

to squint to look at sth with your eyes partly closed, often because the sun is too bright

He glanced up at the cloud, which was close enough to the sun that he had to squint to look at it.

★curiosity the desire to learn more or find out particular information
curious 1. wanting to know more about sth; 2. strange or unusual

to get the better of sb to overcome, win a victory over; here: to cause sb to act in a way they would not normally behave

He dug his shovel back into the earth, scooped out some dirt, and lifted it over his dirt pile. But instead of dumping it there, he tossed it off to the side. His curiosity, had gotten the better of him.

He climbed up out of his hole and sifted his fingers through the pile. He felt something hard and metallic.

He pulled it out. It was a gold tube, about as long and as wide as the second finger on his right hand. The tube was open at one end and closed at the other.

He used a few drops of his precious water to clean it.

There seemed to be some kind of design on the flat, closed end. He poured a few more drops of water on it and rubbed it on the inside of his pants pocket.

He looked again at the design engraved into the flat bottom of the tube. He could see an outline of a heart, with the letters *KB* etched inside it.

to engrave to cut words, names or other designs into metal, wood, glass, etc.

He tried to figure out some way that he wouldn't have to give it to X-Ray. He could just keep it, but that wouldn't do him any good. He wanted a day off.

Do you think the Warden will be interested in the tube?

He looked at the large piles of dirt near where X-Ray was digging. X-Ray was probably almost finished for the day. Getting the rest of the day off would hardly do him much good. X-Ray would first have to show the tube to Mr. Sir or Mr. Pendanski, who would then have to show it to the Warden. By then X-Ray might be done anyway.

to be done to have finished

Stanley wondered about trying to secretly take the tube directly to the Warden. He could explain the situation to the Warden, and the Warden might make up an excuse for giving him the day off, so X-Ray wouldn't suspect.

***to suspect** to distrust sb and think that sth bad has happened or is happening
suspect (noun) sb who is thought to be guilty of a crime
suspect (adj.) appearing to be untrue or dishonest

He looked across the lake toward the cabin under the two oak trees. The place scared him. He'd been at Camp Green Lake almost two weeks, and he still hadn't seen the Warden. That was just as well. If he could go his entire year and a half without seeing the Warden, that would be fine with him.

Besides, he didn't know if the Warden would find the tube "interesting." He looked at it again. It looked familiar. He thought he'd seen something like it, somewhere before, but couldn't quite place it.

***familiar** well-known or easily recognizable because you have seen, heard, or experienced it before

"What you got there, Caveman?" asked Zigzag.

Stanley's large hand closed around the tube. "Nothin', just, uh ..." It was useless. "I think I might have found something."

***useless** not effective
useful helping for doing or getting what you want

"Another fossil?"

"No, I'm not sure what it is."

"Let me see," said Zigzag.

Instead of showing it to Zigzag, Stanley brought it to X-Ray. Zigzag followed.

X-Ray looked at the tube, then rubbed his dirty glasses on his dirty shirt and looked at the tube again. One by one, the other boys dropped their shovels and came to look.

shotgun shell *Schrotpatrone*

"It looks like an old shotgun shell," said Squid.

"Yeah, that's probably what it is," said Stanley. He decided not to mention the engraved design. Maybe nobody would notice it. He doubted X-Ray could see it.

"No, it's too long and thin to be a shotgun shell," said Magnet.

junk old or unwanted objects that have no use or value

"It's prob'ly just a piece of junk", said Stanley.

"Well, I'll show it to Mom," said X-Ray. "See what he thinks. Who knows? Maybe I'll get the day off."

"Your hole's almost finished," said Stanley.

"Yeah, so?"

Stanley raised and lowered his shoulder. "So, why don't you wait until tomorrow to show it to Mom?" he suggested. "You can pretend you found it first thing in the morning. Then you can get the whole day off, instead of just an hour or so this afternoon."

X-Ray smiled. "Good thinking, Caveman." He dropped the tube into his large pocket on the right leg of his dirty orange pants.

Stanley returned to his hole.

When the water truck came, Stanley started to take his place at the end of the line, but X-Ray told him to get behind Magnet, in front of Zero.

Stanley moved up one place in line.

14

That night, as Stanley lay on his scratchy and smelly cot, he tried to figure out what he could have done differently, but there was nothing he could do. For once in his unlucky life, he was in the right place at the right time, and it still didn't help him.

"You got it?" he asked X-Ray the next morning at breakfast.

X-Ray looked at him with half-opened eyes behind his dirty glasses. "I don't know what you're talking about," he grumbled.

"You know ..." said Stanley.

"No, I don't know!" X-Ray snapped. "So just leave me alone, okay? I don't want to talk to you."

to snap to answer abruptly in an angry way

Stanley didn't say another word.

Mr. Sir marched the boys out to the lake, chewing sunflower seeds along the way and spitting out the shells. He scraped the ground with his boot heel, to mark where each boy was supposed to dig.

Stanley stamped down on the back of the blade of the shovel, piercing the hard, dry earth. He couldn't figure out why X-Ray snapped at him. If he wasn't going to produce the tube, why did he make Stanley give it to him? Was he just going to keep it? The tube was gold in color, but Stanley didn't think it was real gold.

The water truck came a little after sunrise. Stanley finished his last drop of water and stepped up out of his hole. At this time of day, Stanley sometimes could see some distant hills or mountains on the other side of the lake. They were only visible for a short while and would soon disappear behind the haze of heat and dirt.

distant far away

haze smoke, dust, or mist in the air which is difficult to see through

The truck stopped, and the dust cloud drifted past it. X-Ray took his place at the front of the line. Mr. Pendanski filled his canteen. "Thanks, Mom," X-Ray said. He didn't mention the tube.

Mr. Pendanski filled all the canteens, then climbed back into the cab of the pickup. He still had to bring water to Group E. Stanley could see them digging about two hundred, yards away.

yard a unit for measuring length, equal to three feet or 0.91 meters. 200 yards are equivalent to about 183 meters.

"Mr. Pendanski!" X-Ray shouted from his hole. "Wait! Mr. Pendanski! I think I might have found something!"

The boys all followed Mr. Pendanski as he walked over to X-Ray's hole. Stanley could see the gold tube sticking out of some dirt on the end of X-Ray's shovel.

Mr. Pendanski examined it and took a long look at its flat bottom. "I think the Warden is going to like this."

"Does X-Ray get the day off?" asked Squid.

"Just keep digging until someone says otherwise," Mr. Pendanski said. Then he smiled. "But if I were you, Rex, I wouldn't dig too hard."

Stanley watched the cloud of dust move across the lake to the cabin beneath the trees.

The boys in Group E were just going to have to wait. It didn't take long for the pickup to return. Mr. Pendanski stepped out of the cab. A tall woman with red hair stepped out of the passenger side. She looked even taller than she was, since Stanley was down in his hole. She wore a black cowboy hat and

cab part of a truck that the driver sits in

studded with decorated with a lot of small jewels
turquoise a valuable greenish-blue stone or a jewel that is made from this
***freckles** small brown spots on sb's skin, typically due to exposure to the sun

***to reward** to give sth nice to sb because they have done sth good or helpful or have earned it
reward sth that you get because you have done sth good or helpful or have worked hard
rewarding giving you a sense of happiness and satisfaction because you feel you are doing sth worthwhile, even if you do not earn much money

to wiggle to move with small movements from side to side or up and down

black cowboy boots which were studded with turquoise stones. The sleeves on her shirt were rolled up, and her arms were covered with freckles, as was her face. She walked right up to X-Ray.

"This where you found it?"

"Yes, ma'am."

"Your good work will be rewarded." She turned to Mr. Pendanski. "Drive X-Ray back to camp. Let him take a double shower, and give him some clean clothes. But first I want you to fill everyone's canteen."

"I just filled them a little while ago," said Mr. Pendanski.

The Warden stared hard at him. "Excuse me," she said. Her voice was soft.

"I had just filled them when Rex –"

"Excuse me," the Warden said again. "Did I ask you when you last filled them?"

"No, but it's just –"

"Excuse me."

Mr. Pendanski stopped talking. The Warden wiggled her finger for him to come to her. "It's hot and it's only going to get hotter," she said. "Now, these fine boys have been working hard. Don't you think it might be possible that they might have taken a drink since you last filled their canteens?"

Mr. Pendanski said nothing.

The Warden turned to Stanley. "Caveman, will you come here, please?"

Stanley was surprised she knew his name. He had never seen her. Until she stepped out of the truck, he didn't even know the Warden was a woman.

He nervously went toward her.

"Mr. Pendanski and I have been having a discussion. Have you taken a drink since Mr. Pendanski last filled your canteen?"

Stanley didn't want to cause any trouble for Mr. Pendanski. "I still got plenty left," he said.

"Excuse me."

He stopped. "Yeah, I drank some."

"Thank you. May I see your canteen please."

Stanley handed it to her. Her fingernails were painted dark red.

She gently shook the canteen, letting the water swish inside the plastic container. "Do you hear the empty spaces?" she asked.

"Yes," said Mr. Pendanski.

"Then fill it," she said. "And the next time I tell you to do something, I expect you to do it without questioning my authority. If it's too much trouble for you to fill a canteen, I'll give you a shovel. You can dig the hole, and the Caveman can fill your canteen." She turned back to Stanley. "I don't think that would be too much trouble for you, would it?"

"No," said Stanley.

"So what will it be?" she asked Mr. Pendanski. "Do you want to fill the canteens or do you want to dig?"

"I'll fill the canteens," said Mr. Pendanski.

"Thank you."

15

Mr. Pendanski filled the canteens.

The Warden got a pitchfork out of the back of the pickup. She poked it through X-Ray's dirt pile, to see if anything else might have been buried in there as well.

pitchfork a farm tool with a long handle and two long curved metal points, used esp. for lifting hay

"After you drop off X-Ray, I want you to bring back three wheelbarrows," she said.

wheelbarrow a small cart with one wheel and two handles that is used outdoors to wheel heavy things from one place to another

X-Ray got in the pickup. As the truck pulled away, he leaned out the wide window and waved.

"Zero," said the Warden. "I want you to take over X-Ray's hole." She seemed to know that Zero was the fastest digger. "Armpit and Squid, you will keep digging where you have been," she said. "But you're each going to have a helper. Zigzag, you help Armpit. Magnet will help Squid. And Caveman, you'll work with Zero. We're going to dig the dirt twice. Zero will dig it out of the hole, and Caveman will carefully shovel it into a wheelbarrow. Zigzag will do the same for Armpit, and the same with Magnet and Squid. We don't want to miss anything. If either of you find something, you'll both get the rest of the day off, and a double shower.

"When the wheelbarrows are full, you are to dump them away from this area. We don't want any dirt piles to get in the way."

The Warden remained at the site for the remainder of the day, along with Mr. Pendanski and Mr. Sir, who showed up after a while. Occasionally Mr. Sir would leave to take water to the other groups of campers, but otherwise he and the water truck stayed parked there. The Warden saw to it that nobody in Group D was ever thirsty.

remainder rest

Stanley did as he was told. He carefully looked through all the dirt dug up by Zero, as he shoveled it into a wheelbarrow, though he knew he wouldn't find anything.

distance the amount of space between two places or things

It was easier than digging his own hole. When the wheelbarrow was full, he took it a good distance away before dumping it.

The Warden couldn't keep still. She kept walking around, looking over the boys' shoulders, and sticking her pitchfork through the dirt piles. "You're doing fine, just fine," she told Stanley.

After a while, she told the boys to switch places, so that Stanley Zigzag, and Magnet dug in the holes, and Zero, Armpit, and Squid shoveled the excavated dirt into the wheelbarrows.

After lunch, Zero took over the digging again, and Stanley returned to the wheelbarrow. "There's no hurry" the Warden said several times. "The main thing is not to miss anything."

six feet about 183 centimeters

The boys dug until each hole was well over six feet deep and wide. Still, it was easier for two boys to dig a six-foot hole than it was for one boy to dig a five-foot hole.

"All right, that's enough for today," the Warden said. "I've waited this long, I can wait another day."

Mr. Sir drove her back to her cabin.

"I wonder how she knew all our names," Stanley said as he walked back to the compound.

"She watches us all the time," said Zigzag. "She's got hidden microphones and cameras all over the place. In the tents, the Wreck Room, the shower."

paranoid believing irrationally that you cannot trust other people because they are trying to harm you or have a bad opinion of you

"The shower?" asked Stanley. He wondered if Zigzag was just being paranoid.

"The cameras are tiny," said Armpit. "No bigger than the toenail on your little toe."

Stanley had his doubts about that. He didn't think they could make cameras that small. Microphones, maybe.

He realized that was why X-Ray didn't want to talk to him about the gold tube at breakfast. X-Ray was afraid the Warden might have been listening.

What are they looking for? ➔ Take a guess.

One thing was certain: They weren't just digging to "build character." They were definitely looking for something.

And whatever they were looking for, they were looking in the wrong place.

to gaze at to look at sb or sth for a long time, often without realizing it; stare

Stanley gazed out across the lake, toward the spot where he had been digging yesterday when he found the gold tube. He dug the hole into his memory.

16

As Stanley entered the Wreck Room, he could hear X-Ray's voice from all the way across the room.

"See what I'm saying," X-Ray said. "Am I right, or am I right?"

The other bodies in the room were little more than bags of flesh and bones, dumped across broken chairs and couches. X-Ray was full of life, laughing and waving his arms around as he talked. "Yo, Caveman, my man!" he called out.

Stanley made his way across the room.

"Hey, slide on over, Squid," said X-Ray. "Make room for the Caveman."

Stanley crashed on the couch.

He had looked for a hidden camera in the shower. He hadn't seen anything, and he hoped the Warden hadn't either.

"What's the matter?" asked X-Ray. "You guys tired or something?" He laughed.

"Hey, keep it down, will you," groaned Zigzag. "I'm trying to watch TV."

Stanley glanced uncertainly at Zigzag, who was staring very intently at the busted television screen.

The Warden greeted the boys at breakfast the next morning and went with them to the holes. Four dug in the holes, and three tended to the wheelbarrows. "Glad you're here, X-Ray," she said to him. "We need your sharp eyes."

Stanley spent more time pushing the wheelbarrow than digging, because he was such a slow digger. He carted away the excess dirt and dumped it into previously dug holes. He was careful not to dump any of it in the hole where the gold tube was actually found.

He could still see the tube in his mind. It seemed so familiar, but he just couldn't place it. He thought that it might have been the lid to a fancy gold pen. *KB* could have been the initials of a famous author. The only famous authors he could think of were Charles Dickens, William Shakespeare, and Mark Twain. Besides, it didn't really look like the top of a pen.

By lunchtime the Warden was beginning to lose her patience. She made them eat quickly, so they could get back to work. "If you can't get them to work any faster," she told Mr. Sir, "then you're going to have to climb down there and dig with them."

After that, everyone worked faster, especially when Mr. Sir was watching them. Stanley practically ran when he pushed

busted *(infml)* broken
to tend to sth to look after sth
excess not needed because there is enough of sth already
previously before now or before a particular time
lid a cover for a container

Charles Dickens (1812–70) a British writer whose novels made him the most popular British writer of the 19th century. His books, which are still popular today, contain humorous characters with unusual names, many of which have become well-known in their own right. Nevertheless, his books also show how hard life was in Victorian England, especially for poor people and children. His most famous works include *David Copperfield*, *Oliver Twist*, *Great Expectations*, and *A Christmas Carol*.
William Shakespeare (1564–1616) an English writer, who most people regard as the greatest of all English writers. His many famous plays include the tragedies *Romeo and Juliet*, *Hamlet* and *Macbeth*; the comedies *A Midsummer Night's Dream* and *As You Like It*; and the historical plays *Richard III* and *Henry V*. He also wrote poetry, including the Sonnets, and worked as an actor at the Globe Theatre in London.
Mark Twain (1835–1910) a U.S. writer best known for his novels *The Adventures of Tom Sawyer* and *The Adventures of Huckleberry Finn*, and for his descriptions of life on the Mississippi River. His real name was Samuel Langhorne Clemens.

patience the ability to continue waiting for or doing sth for a long time without becoming angry or nervous

his wheelbarrow. Mr. Sir reminded them that they weren't Girl Scouts.

They didn't quit digging until after every other group had finished.

Later, as Stanley sat sprawled across an understuffed chair, he tried to think of a way to tell the Warden where the tube was really found, without getting himself or X-Ray into trouble. It didn't seem possible. He even thought about sneaking out at night and digging in that hole by himself. But the last thing he wanted to do after digging all day was to dig at night, too. Besides, the shovels were locked up at night, presumably so they couldn't be used as weapons.

to sneak out to go somewhere secretly and quietly in order to avoid being seen or heard; to creep

Mr. Pendanski entered the Wreck Room. "Stanley," he called as he made his way to him.

"His name's Caveman," said X-Ray.

"Stanley," said Mr. Pendanski.

"My name's Caveman," said Stanley.

"Well, I have a letter here for someone named Stanley Yelnats," said Mr. Pendanski. He turned over an envelope his hands. "It doesn't say Caveman anywhere."

***envelope** a thin paper cover that you put a letter in before sending it

"Uh, thanks," Stanley said, taking it.

It was from his mother.

"Who's it from?" Squid asked. "Your *mother*?"

Stanley put it in the big pocket of his pants.

"Aren't you going to read it to us?" asked Armpit.

"Give him some space," said X-Ray. "If Caveman doesn't want to read it to us, he doesn't have to. It's probably from his girlfriend."

Stanley smiled.

He read it later, after the other boys had gone to dinner.

Dear Stanley,

It was wonderful to hear from you. Your letter made me feel like one of the other moms who can afford to send their kids to summer camp. I know it's not the same, but I am very proud of you for trying to make the best of a bad situation. Who knows? Maybe something good will come of this.

Your father thinks he is real close to a breakthrough on his sneaker project. I hope so. The landlord is threatening to evict us because of the odor.

I feel sorry for the little old lady who lived in a shoe. It must have smelled awful!

Love from both of us,

***landlord (landlady)** a man (woman) who rents out a room, building or piece of land to sb

to evict sb to legally force sb to leave the house they are living in, esp. if they do not own it

"What's so funny?" Zero asked.

It startled him. He thought Zero had gone to dinner with the others.

"Nothing. Just something my mom wrote."

"What'd she say?" Zero asked.

"Nothing."

"Oh, sorry," said Zero.

"Well, see my dad is trying to invent a way to recycle old sneakers. So the apartment kind of smells bad, because he's always cooking these old sneakers. So anyway, in the letter my mom said she felt sorry for that little old lady who lived in a shoe, you know, because it must have smelled bad in there."

Zero stared blankly at him.

"You know, the nursery rhyme?"

Zero said nothing.

"You've heard the nursery rhyme about the little old lady who lived in a shoe?"

"No."

Stanley was amazed.

"How does it go?" asked Zero.

"Didn't you ever watch *Sesame Street*?" Stanley asked.

Zero stared blankly.

Stanley headed on to dinner. He would have felt pretty silly reciting nursery rhymes at Camp Green Lake.

to startle sb to surprise sb by appearing unexpectedly

blankly in a way that shows no emotion, understanding, or interest

nursery rhyme a short, traditional poem or song for children

***amazed** very surprised
amazing very good, esp. in an unexpected way
amazement a feeling of great surprise

Sesame Street one of the most popular and well-respected television shows for young children that originated in the U.S., but has since spread worldwide. It teaches children about words, numbers and the alphabet in an amusing way, but also deals with important social issues, such as racism and attitudes towards people who are disabled.

to recite to say a poem, piece of literature, etc. that you have learned off by heart for people to listen to

The most common version of the nursery rhyme is:

> There was an old woman
> who lived in a shoe.
> She had so many
> children, she didn't know
> what to do.
> She gave them some
> broth without any bread;
> Then whipped them all
> soundly and put them to
> bed.

17

For the next week and a half, the boys continued to dig in and around the area where X-Ray had supposedly found the gold tube. They widened X-Ray's hole, as well as the holes Armpit and Squid had been digging, until the fourth day, when all three holes met and formed one big hole.

As the days wore on, the Warden became less and less patient. She arrived later in the morning and left earlier in the afternoon. Meanwhile, the boys continued to dig later and later.

"This is no bigger than it was when I left you yesterday," she said after arriving late one morning, well after sunrise. "What have you been doing down there?"

"Nothing," said Squid.

It was the wrong thing to say.

At just that moment, Armpit was returning from a bathroom break.

"How nice of you to join us," she said. "And what have you been doing?"

"I had to ... you know ... go."

The Warden jabbed at Armpit with her pitchfork, knocking him backward into the big hole. The pitchfork left three holes in the front of his shirt, and three tiny spots of blood.

"You're giving these boys too much water," the Warden told Mr. Pendanski.

They continued to dig until late afternoon, long after all the other groups had finished for the day. Stanley was down in the big hole, along with the other six boys. They had stopped using the wheelbarrows.

He dug his shovel into the side of the hole. He scooped up some dirt, and was raising it up to the surface when Zigzag's shovel caught him in the side of the head.

He collapsed.

to pass out to faint; to become unconscious
ain't *(infml)* am not

He wasn't sure if he passed our or not. He looked up to see Zigzag's wild head staring down at him. "I ain't digging that dirt up," Zigzag said. "That's your dirt."

"Hey, Mom!" Magnet called. "Caveman's been hurt."

gash a large deep cut

Stanley brought his fingers up the side of his neck. He felt his wet blood and a pretty big gash just below his ear.

nap a short sleep

Magnet helped Stanley to his feet, then up and out of the hole. Mr. Sir made a bandage out of a piece of his sack of sunflower seeds and taped it over Stanley's wound. Then he told him to get back to work. "It isn't nap time."

When Stanley returned to the hole, Zigzag was waiting for him.

"That's your dirt," Zigzag said. "You have to dig it up. It's covering up my dirt."

Stanley felt a little dizzy. He could see a small pile of dirt. It took him a moment to realize that it was the dirt which had been on his shovel when he was hit.

He scooped it up, then Zigzag dug his shovel into the ground underneath where "Stanley's dirt" had been.

18

The next morning Mr. Sir marched the boys to another section of the lake, and each boy dug his own hole, five feet deep and five feet wide. Stanley was glad to be away from the big hole. At least now he knew just how much he had to dig for the day. And it was a relief not to have other shovels swinging past his face, or the Warden hanging around.

five feet are equivalent to about 152 centimetres

He dug his shovel into the dirt, then slowly turned to dump it into a pile. He had to make his turns smooth and slow. If he jerked too quickly, he felt a throbbing pain just above his neck where Zigzag's shovel had hit him.

That part of his head, between his neck and ear, was considerably swollen. There were no mirrors in camp, but he imagined he looked like he had a hard-boiled egg sticking out of him.

considerably quite a bit

The remainder of his body hardly hurt at all. His muscles had strengthened, and his hands were tough and callused. He was still the slowest digger, but not all that much slower than Magnet. Less than thirty minutes after Magnet returned to camp, Stanley spat into his hole.

callused *schwielig*

After his shower, he put his dirty clothes in his crate and got out his box of stationery. He stayed in the tent to write the letter so Squid and the other boys wouldn't make fun of him for writing to his mother.

Dear Mom and Dad,

Camp is hard, but challenging. We've been running obstacle courses, and have to swim long distances on the lake. Tomorrow we learn

obstacle course line of objects which people or animals have to jump over, climb through, etc., typically under time pressure or in a race

He stopped writing as Zero walked into the tent, then returned to his letter. He didn't care what Zero thought. Zero was nobody.

to rock climb. I know that sounds scary, but don't worry,

Zero was standing beside him now, watching him write.

Stanley turned, and felt his neck throb. "I don't like it when you read over my shoulder, okay?" Zero said nothing.

to throb here: to beat painfully with a strong, regular rhythm

I'll be careful. It's not all fun and games here, but I think I'm getting a lot out of it. It builds character. The other boys

"I don't know how," said Zero.

"What?"

"Can you teach me?"

Stanley didn't know what he was talking about. "Teach you what, to rock climb?"

Zero stared at him with penetrating eyes.

sore hurting; in pain

"What?" said Stanley. He was hot, tired, and sore.

Why does Zero want to learn how to read?

"I want to learn to read and write," said Zero.

Stanley let out a short laugh. He wasn't laughing at Zero. He was just surprised. All this time he had thought Zero was reading over his shoulder. "Sorry," he said. "I don't know how to teach."

After digging all day, he didn't have the strength to try to teach Zero to read and write. He needed to save his energy for the people who counted.

to count here: to matter, to be important

"You don't have to teach me to write," said Zero. "Just to read. I don't have anybody to write to."

"Sorry," Stanley said again.

His muscles and hands weren't the only parts of his body that had toughened over the past several weeks. His heart had hardened as well.

to toughen to make sb or sth stronger

He finished his letter. He barely had enough moisture in his mouth to seal and stamp the envelope. It seemed that no matter how much water he drank, he was always thirsty.

19

He was awakened one night by a strange noise. At first he thought it might have been some kind of animal, and it frightened him. But as the sleep cleared from his head, he realized that the noise was coming from the cot next to him. Squid was crying.

"You okay?" Stanley whispered.

to whisper to talk in a soft, low voice so that other people cannot hear you well

to jerk to make a sudden, quick movement

Squid's head jerked around. He sniffed and caught his breath.

"Yeah, I just … I'm fine," he whispered, and sniffed again.

In the morning Stanley asked Squid if he was feeling better.

"What are you, my mother?" asked Squid.

Stanley raised and lowered one shoulder.

"I got allergies, okay?" Squid said.

"Okay," said Stanley.

jaw *Kiefer*

"You open your mouth again, and I'll break your jaw."

***

Stanley kept his mouth shut most of the time. He didn't talk too much to any of the boys, afraid that he might say the wrong thing. They called him Caveman and all that, but he couldn't forget that they were dangerous, too. They were all here for a reason. As Mr. Sir would say, this wasn't a Girl Scout camp.

Stanley was thankful that there were no racial problems. X-Ray, Armpit, and Zero were black. He, Squid, and Zigzag were white. Magnet was Hispanic. On the lake they were all the same reddish brown color – the color of dirt.

Hispanic from countries where Spanish or Portuguese are spoken

He looked up from his hole to see the water truck and its trailing dust cloud. His canteen was still almost a quarter full. He quickly drank it down, then took his place in line, behind Magnet and in front of Zero. The air was thick with heat, dust, and exhaust fumes.

exhaust fumes the poisonous waste gases that come from cars, trucks, etc.

Mr. Sir filled their canteens.

The truck pulled away. Stanley was back in his hole, shovel in hand, when he heard Magnet call out. "Anybody want some sunflower seeds?"

Magnet was standing at ground level, holding a sack of seeds. He popped a handful into his mouth, chewed, and swallowed, shells and all.

"Over here," called X-Ray.

The sack looked to be about half full. Magnet rolled up the top, then tossed it to X-Ray.

"How'd you get them without Mr. Sir seeing you?" asked Armpit.

"I can't help it," Magnet said. He held both hands up, wiggled his fingers, and laughed. "My fingers are like little magnets."

The sack went from X-Ray to Armpit to Squid.

"It's sure good to eat something that doesn't come from a can," said Armpit.

Squid tossed the sack to Zigzag.

Stanley knew it would come to him next. He didn't even want it. From the moment Magnet shouted, "Anybody want some sunflower seeds," he knew there would be trouble. Mr. Sir was sure to come back. And anyway, the salted shells would only make him thirsty.

"Coming your way, Caveman," said Zigzag. "Airmail and special delivery ..."

It's unclear whether the seeds spilled before they got to Stanley or after he dropped the bag. It seemed to him that Zigzag

to spill to accidentally flow over the edge of a container

to sweep to push sth from one place to another using a brush, broom or your hand

judge here: sb who decides the value or quality of sth

burlap *Jute*

hadn't rolled up the top before throwing it, and that was the reason he didn't catch it.

But it all happened very fast. One moment the sack was flying through the air, and the next thing Stanley knew the sack was in his hole and the seeds were spilled across the dirt.

"Oh, man!" said Magnet.

"Sorry," Stanley said as he tried to sweep the seeds back into the sack.

"I don't want to eat dirt," said X-Ray.

Stanley didn't know what to do.

"The truck's coming!" shouted Zigzag.

Stanley looked up at the approaching dust cloud, then back down at the spilled seeds. He was in the wrong place at the wrong time.

What else is new?

He dug his shovel into his hole, and tried to turn over the dirt and bury the seeds.

What he should have done, he realized later, was knock one of his dirt piles back into his hole. But the idea of putting dirt *into* his hole was unthinkable.

"Hello, Mr. Sir," said X-Ray. "Back so soon?"

"It seems like you were just here," said Armpit.

"Time flies when you're having fun," said Magnet.

Stanley continued to turn the dirt over in his hole.

"You Girl Scouts having a good time?" asked Mr. Sir. He moved from one hole to another. He kicked a dirt pile by Magnet's hole, then he moved toward Stanley.

Stanley could see two seeds at the bottom of his hole. As he tried to cover them up, he unearthed a corner of the sack.

"Well, what do you know, Caveman?" said Mr. Sir, standing over him. "It looks like you found something."

Stanley didn't know what to do.

"Dig it out," Mr. Sir said. "We'll take it to the Warden. Maybe she'll give you the rest of the day off."

"It's not anything," Stanley muttered.

"Let me be the judge of that," said Mr. Sir.

Stanley reached down and pulled up the empty burlap sack. He tried to hand it to Mr. Sir, but he wouldn't take it.

"So, tell me, Caveman," said Mr. Sir. "How did my sack of sunflower seeds get in your hole?"

"I stole it from your truck."

"You did?"

"Yes, Mr. Sir."

"What happened to all the sunflower seeds?"

"I ate them."

"By yourself."

"Yes, Mr. Sir."

"Hey, Caveman!" shouted Armpit. "How come you didn't share any with us?"

"That's cold, man," said X-Ray.

"I thought you were our friend," said Magnet.

Mr. Sir looked around from one boy to another, then back to Stanley. "We'll see what the Warden has to say about this. Let's go."

Stanley climbed up out of his hole and followed Mr. Sir to the truck. He still held the empty sack.

It felt good to sit inside the truck, out of the direct rays of the sun. Stanley was surprised he could feel good about anything at the moment, but he did. It felt good to sit down on a comfortable seat for a change. And as the truck bounced along the dirt, he was able to appreciate the air blowing through the open window onto his hot and sweaty face.

cold here: unkind, mean

to bounce here: to move up and down in an erratic way

to appreciate to recognize the value of sth

20

It felt good to walk in the shade of the two oak trees. Stanley wondered if this was how a condemned man felt on his way to the electric chair – appreciating all of the good things in life for the last time.

They had to step around holes to get to the cabin door. Stanley was surprised to see so many around the cabin. He would have expected the Warden to not want the campers digging so close to her home. But several holes were right up against the cabin wall. The holes were closer together here as well, and were of different shapes and sizes.

Mr. Sir knocked on the door. Stanley still held the empty sack.

"Yes?" the Warden said, opening the door.

"There's been a little trouble out on the lake," Mr. Sir said. "Caveman will tell you all about it."

The Warden stared at Mr. Sir a moment, then her gaze turned toward Stanley. He felt nothing but dread now.

"Come in, I suppose," said the Warden. "You're letting the cold out."

It was air-conditioned inside her cabin. The television was going. She picked up the remote and turned it off.

condemned here: sentenced to death for a serious crime

dread strong fear and bad feelings about an upcoming event

remote remote control; *Fernbedienung*

She sat down on a canvas chair. She was barefoot and wearing shorts. Her legs were as freckled as her face and arms.

"So what is it you have to tell me?"

Stanley took a breath to steady himself. "While Mr. Sir was filling the canteens, I snuck into the truck and stole his sack of sunflower seeds."

to sneak, snuck, snuck to go quietly and secretly

"I see." She turned to Mr. Sir. "That's why you brought him here?"

"Yes, but I think he's lying. I think someone else stole the sack, and Caveman is covering up for X-Ray or somebody. It was a twenty-pound sack, and he claims to have eaten them all by himself." He took the sack from Stanley and handed it to the Warden.

twenty pound about nine kilograms

"I see," the Warden said again.

"The sack wasn't full," said Stanley. "And I spilled a lot. You can check my hole."

In that room, Caveman, there's a small flowered case. Will you get it for me, please?" She pointed to a door.

Stanley looked at the door, then at the Warden, then back at the door. He slowly walked toward it.

It was a kind of dressing room, with a sink and a mirror. Next to the sink he saw the case, white with pink roses.

sink a basin for washing your hands

He brought it back out to the Warden, and she set it on the glass coffee table in front of her. She unclasped the latch and opened the case.

It was a makeup case. Stanley's mother had one similar to it. He saw several bottles of nail polish, polish remover, a couple of lipstick tubes, and other jars and powders.

The Warden held up a small jar of dark-red nail polish. "You see this, Caveman?"

He nodded.

"This is my special nail polish. Do you see the dark rich color? You can't buy that in a store. I have to make it myself."

Stanley had no idea why she was showing it to him. He wondered why the Warden would ever have the need to wear nail polish or makeup.

"Do you want to know my secret ingredient?"

ingredient *Zutat*

He raised and lowered one shoulder.

The Warden opened the bottle. "Rattlesnake venom." With a small paintbrush she began applying it to the nails on her left hand. "It's perfectly harmless ... when it's dry."

venom poisonous liquid produced by snakes and various other animals to kill their prey

She finished her left hand. She waved it in the air for a few seconds, then began painting the nails on her right hand. "It's only toxic while it's wet."

toxic poisonous

She finished painting her nails, then stood up. She reached over and touched Stanley's face with her fingers. She ran her sharp wet nails very gently down his cheek. He felt his skin tingle.

The nail on her pinkie just barely touched the wound behind his ear. A sharp sting of pain caused him to jump back.

The Warden turned to face Mr. Sir, who was sitting on the fireplace hearth.

"So you think he stole your sunflower seeds?"

"No, he says he stole them, but I think it was –"

She stepped toward him and struck him across the face.

Mr. Sir stared at her. He had three long red marks slanting across the left side of his face. Stanley didn't know if the redness was caused by her nail polish or his blood.

It took a moment for the venom to sink in. Suddenly, Mr. Sir screamed and clutched his face with both hands. He let himself fall over, rolling off the hearth and onto the rug.

The Warden spoke softly. "I don't especially care about your sunflower seeds."

Mr. Sir moaned.

"If you must know," said the Warden, "I liked it better when you smoked."

For a second, Mr. Sir's pain seemed to recede. He took several long, deep breaths. Then his head jerked violently, and he let out a shrill scream, worse than the one before.

The Warden turned to Stanley. "I suggest you go back to your hole now."

Stanley started to go, but Mr. Sir lay in the way. Stanley could see the muscles on his face jump and twitch. His body writhed in agony.

Stanley stepped carefully over him. "Is he –?"

"Excuse me?" said the Warden.

Stanley was too frightened to speak.

"He's not going to die," the Warden said. "Unfortunately for you."

to tingle to feel as if a lot of small sharp points are pushing into your body
pinkie the smallest finger
hearth floor at the bottom of a fireplace
to slant *schräg sein*
to clutch to grip or hold tightly and firmly
to recede here: to become less intense
to writhe to twist your body without stopping
agony extreme pain

21

It was a long walk back to his hole. Stanley looked out through the haze of heat and dirt at the other boys, lowering and raising their shovels. Group D was the farthest away.

to recover to get back to your normal state of health

He realized that once again he would be digging long after everyone else had quit. He hoped he'd finish before Mr. Sir recovered. He didn't want to be out there alone with Mr. Sir.

He won't die, the Warden had said. *Unfortunately for you.*

Walking across the desolate wasteland, Stanley thought about his great-grandfather – not the pig stealer but the pig stealer's son, the one who was robbed by Kissin' Kate Barlow.

He tried to imagine how he must have felt after Kissin' Kate had left him stranded in the desert. It probably wasn't a whole lot different from the way he himself felt now. Kate Barlow had left his great-grandfather to face the hot barren desert. The Warden had left Stanley to face Mr. Sir.

insane crazy

refuge shelter or protection from danger
to take/seek refuge in sth to use a place as a shelter or protection from danger
refugee sb who has been forced to leave their country to escape war, hunger, persecution or a natural disaster
refugee camps temporary accommodation for refugee seekers until they can find somewhere else to live

Somehow his great-grandfather had survived for seventeen days, before he was rescued by a couple of rattlesnake hunters. He was insane when they found him.

When he was asked how he had lived so long, he said he "found refuge on God's thumb."

He spent nearly a month in a hospital. He ended up marrying one of the nurses. Nobody ever knew what he meant by God's thumb, including himself.

Stanley heard a twitching sound. He stopped in mid-step, with one foot still in the air.

to coil to wind into a series of circles

A rattlesnake lay coiled beneath his foot. Its tail was pointed upward, rattling.

Stanley backed his leg away, then turned and ran.

The rattlesnake didn't chase after him. It had rattled its tail to warn him to stay away.

"Thanks for the warning," Stanley whispered as his heart pounded.

The rattlesnake would be a lot more dangerous if it didn't have a rattle.

"Hey, Caveman!" called Armpit. "You're still alive."

"What'd the Warden say?" asked X-Ray.

"What'd you tell her?" asked Magnet.

"I told her I stole the seeds," said Stanley.

"Good going," said Magnet.

"What'd she do?" asked Zigzag.

Stanley shrugged one shoulder. "Nothing. She got mad at Mr. Sir for bothering her."

He didn't feel like going into details. If he didn't talk about it, then maybe it didn't happen.

He went over to his hole, and to his surprise it was nearly finished. He stared at it, amazed. It didn't make sense.

Or perhaps it did. He smiled. Since he had taken the blame for the sunflower seeds, he realized, the other boys had dug his hole for him.

"Hey, thanks," he said.

"Don't look at me," said X-Ray.

Confused, Stanley looked around – from Magnet, to Armpit, to Zigzag, to Squid. None of them took credit for it.

Then he turned to Zero, who had been quietly digging in his hole since Stanley's return. Zero's hole was smaller than all the others.

to take credit for sth to allow people to believe that one has done sth praiseworthy

22

Stanley was the first one finished. He spat in his hole, then showered and changed into his cleaner set of clothes. It had been three days since the laundry was done, so even his clean set was dirty and smelly. Tomorrow, these would become his work clothes, and his other set would be washed.

He could think of no reason why Zero would dig his hole for him. Zero didn't even get any sunflower seeds.

"I guess he likes to dig holes," Armpit had said.

"He's a mole", Zigzag had said. "I think he eats dirt."

"Moles don't eat dirt," X-Ray had pointed out. "'Worms eat dirt."

"Hey, Zero?" Squid had asked. "Are you a mole or a worm?

Zero had said nothing.

Stanley never even thanked him. But now he sat on his cot and waited for Zero to return from the shower room.

"Thanks," he said as Zero entered through the tent flap.

Zero glanced at him, then went over to the crates, where he deposited his dirty clothes and towel.

"Why'd you help me?" Stanley asked.

Zero turned around. "You didn't steal the sunflower seeds," he said.

"So, neither did you," said Stanley.

Zero stared at him. His eyes seemed to expand, and it was almost as if Zero were looking right through him. "You didn't steal the sneakers," he said.

Stanley said nothing.

He watched Zero walk out of the tent. If anybody had X-ray vision, it was Zero.

* **laundry** dirty clothes that need washing

mole *Maulwurf*

to expand to become larger in size, number, or amount
to expand on to provide more facts and details about sth that you have already mentioned in general
expanding increasing in size, number or amount; e.g. a rapidly-expanding labour force
expanse a large continuous area, esp. land, sky or water

"Wait!" he called, then hurried out after him.

Zero had stopped just outside the tent, and Stanley almost ran into him.

"I'll try to teach you to read if you want," Stanley offered. "I don't know if I know how to teach, but I'm not that worn out today, since you dug a lot of my hole."

A big smile spread across Zero's face.

They returned to the tent, where they were less likely to be bothered. Stanley got his box of stationery and a pen out of his crate. They sat on the ground.

* **to bother** to annoy, worry or interrupt sb

"Do you know the alphabet?" Stanley asked.

For a second, he thought he saw a flash of defiance in Zero's eyes, but then it passed.

defiance behaviour that shows you refuse to do what sb tells you to do

"I think I know some of it," Zero said. "A, B, C, D."

"Keep going," said Stanley.

Zero's eyes looked upward. "E ..."

"F", said Stanley.

"G," said Zero. He blew some air out of the side of his mouth. "H ... I ... K, P."

"H, I, J, K, L," Stanley said.

"That's right," said Zero. "I've heard it before. I just don't have it memorized exactly."

"That's all right," said Stanley. "Here, I'll say the whole thing, just to kind of refresh your memory, then you can try it."

He recited the alphabet for Zero, then Zero repeated it without a single mistake.

Not bad for a kid who had never seen *Sesame Street*!

"Well, I've heard it before, somewhere," Zero said, trying to act like it was nothing, but his big smile gave him away.

The next step was harder. Stanley had to figure out how to teach him to recognize each letter. He gave Zero a piece of paper, and took a piece for himself. "I guess we'll start with A."

He printed a capital A, and then Zero copied it on his sheet of paper. The paper wasn't lined, which made it more difficult, but Zero's A wasn't bad, just a little big. Stanley told him he needed to write smaller, or else they'd run out of paper real quick. Zero printed it smaller.

capital here: *Großbuchstabe*

"Actually, there are two ways to write each letter," Stanley said, as he realized this was going to be even harder than he thought. "That's a capital A. But usually you'll see a small a. You only have capitals at the beginning of a word, and only if it's the start of a sentence, or if it's a proper noun, like a name."

proper noun *Eigenname*

Zero nodded as if he understand, but Stanley knew he had made very little sense.

He printed a lowercase a, and Zero copied it.

"So there are fifty-two," said Zero.

Stanley didn't know what he was talking about.

"Instead of twenty-six letters. There are really fifty-two."

Stanley looked at him, surprised. "I guess that's right. How'd you figure that out?" he asked.

Zero said nothing.

"Did you add?"

Zero said nothing.

"Did you multiply?"

"That's just how many there are," said Zero.

Stanley raised and lowered one shoulder. He didn't even know how Zero knew there were twenty-six in the first place. Did he count them as he recited them?

He had Zero write a few more upper- and lowercase A's, and then he moved on to a capital B. This was going to take a long time, he realized.

"You can teach me ten letters a day," suggested Zero. "Five capitals and five smalls. After five days I'll know them all. Except on the last day I'll have to do twelve. Six capitals and six smalls."

Again Stanley stared at him, amazed that he was able to figure all that out.

Zero must have thought he was staring for a different reason, because he said, "I'll dig part of your hole every day. I can dig for about an hour, then you can teach me for an hour. And since I'm a faster digger anyway, our holes will get done about the same time. I won't have to wait for you."

"Okay," Stanley agreed.

As Zero was printing his B's, Stanley asked him how he figured out it would take five days. "Did you multiply? Did you divide?"

"That's just what it is," Zero said.

"It's good math," said Stanley.

"I'm not stupid," Zero said. "I know everybody thinks I am. I just don't like answering their questions."

Later that night, as he lay on his cot, Stanley reconsidered the deal he had made with Zero. Getting a break every day would be a relief, but he knew X-Ray wouldn't like it. He wondered if there might be some way Zero would agree to dig part of X-Ray's hole as well. But then again, why should he? *I'm the one teaching Zero. I need the break so I'll have the energy to teach him. I'm the one who took the blame or the sunflower seeds. I'm the one who Mr. Sir is mad at.*

lowercase *Kleinbuchstabe*

to figure sth out to think about a problem until you find the answer

to reconsider to think again about sth to decide if you should perhaps change your mind

to take the blame for sth to accept the responsibility for sth that has gone wrong

He closed his eyes, and images from the Warden's cabin floated inside his head: her red fingernails, Mr. Sir writhing on the floor, her flowered makeup kit.
He opened his eyes.
He suddenly realized where he'd seen the gold tube before. He'd seen it in his mother's bathroom, and he'd seen it again in the Warden's cabin. It was half of a lipstick container.
KB?

KB?
He felt a jolt of astonishment.
His mouth silently formed the name Kate Barlow, as he wondered if it really could have belonged to the kissin' outlaw.

jolt an emotional shock
astonishment extreme surprise or amazement

23

One hundred and ten years ago, Green Lake was the largest lake in Texas. It was full of clear cool water, and it sparkled like a giant emerald in the sun. It was especially beautiful in the spring, when the peach trees, which lined the shore, bloomed with pink and rose-colored blossoms.

emerald *Smaragd*

There was always a town picnic on the Fourth of July. They'd play games, dance, sing, and swim in the lake to keep cool. Prizes were awarded for the best peach pie and peach jam.
A special prize was given every year to Miss Katherine Barlow for her fabulous spiced peaches. No one else even tried to make spiced peaches, because they knew none could be as delicious as hers.
Every summer Miss Katherine would pick bushels of peaches and preserve them in jars with cinnamon, cloves, nutmeg, and other spices which she kept secret.
The jarred peaches would last all winter. They probably would have lasted a lot longer than that, but they were always eaten by the end of winter.

jar a cylindrical glass container with a lid
cinnamon *Zimt*
clove *Nelke*
nutmeg *Muskatnuss*

It was said that Green Lake was "heaven on earth" and that Miss Katherine's spiced peaches were "food for the angels."

Katherine Barlow was the town's only schoolteacher. She taught in an old one-room schoolhouse. It was old even then. The roof leaked. The windows wouldn't open. The door hung crooked on its bent hinges.

She was a wonderful teacher, full of knowledge and full of life. The children loved her.

She taught classes in the evening for adults, and many of the adults loved her as well. She was very pretty. Her classes were often full of young men, who were a lot more interested in the teacher than they were in getting an education.

But all they ever got was an education.

One such young man was Trout Walker. His real name was Charles Walker, but everyone called him Trout because his two feet smelled like a couple of dead fish.

This wasn't entirely Trout's fault. He had an incurable foot fungus. In fact, it was the same foot fungus that a hundred and ten years later would afflict the famous ballplayer Clyde Livingston. But at least Clyde Livingston showered every day.

"I take a bath every Sunday morning," Trout would brag, "whether I need to or not."

Most everyone in the town of Green Lake expected Miss Katherine to marry Trout Walker. He was the son of the richest man in the country. His family owned most of the peach trees and all the land on the east side of the lake.

Trout often showed up at night school but never paid attention. He talked in class and was disrespectful of the students around him. He was loud and stupid.

A lot of men in town were not educated. That didn't bother Miss Katherine. She knew they'd spent most of their lives working on farms and ranches and hadn't had much schooling. That was why she was there – to teach them.

But Trout didn't want to learn. He seemed to be proud of his stupidity.

"How'd you like to take a ride on my new boat this Saturday?" he asked her one evening after class.

"No, thank you," said Miss Katherine.

"We've got a brand-new boat," he said. "You don't even have to row it."

"Yes, I know," said Miss Katherine.

Everyone in town had seen – and heard – the Walkers' new boat. It made a horrible loud noise and spewed ugly black smoke over the beautiful lake.

to leak to allow liquid, gas, etc. to get in or out through a small hole or crack
crooked *schief*
bent *verbogen*
hinge *Scharnier*

trout *Forelle*

fungus *Pilz*
to afflict to affect in an unpleasant way

* **to brag** to say sth in an arrogant way

to bother here: to trouble, worry or distress sb

to spew to cause to flow in large amounts

Trout had always gotten everything he ever wanted. He found it hard to believe that Miss Katherine had turned him down. He pointed his finger at her and said, "No one ever says 'No' to Charles Walker!"
"I believe I just did," said Katherine Barlow.

24

cantaloupe a melon with orange flesh
jagged having a rough edge

oatmeal *Haferflocken*

to choke to prevent sb from breathing by putting your hands around their neck and pressing on it

handsome attractive, good-looking (typically used for men)

Stanley was half asleep as he got in line for breakfast, but the sight of Mr. Sir awakened him. The left side of Mr. Sir's face had swollen to the size of half a cantaloupe. There were three dark-purple jagged lines running down his cheek where the Warden had scratched him.
The other boys in Stanley's tent had obviously seen Mr. Sir as well, but they had the good sense not to say anything. Stanley put a carton of juice and a plastic spoon on his tray. He kept his eyes down and hardly breathed as Mr. Sir ladled some oatmeal-like stuff into his bowl.
He brought his tray to the table. Behind him, a boy from one of the other tents said, "Hey, what happened to your face?"
There was a crash.
Stanley turned to see Mr. Sir holding the boy's head against the oatmeal pot. "Is something wrong with my face?"
The boy tried to speak but couldn't. Mr. Sir had him by the throat.
"Does anyone see anything wrong with my face?" asked Mr. Sir, as he continued to choke the boy.
Nobody said anything.
Mr. Sir let the boy go. His head banged against the table as he fell to the ground.
Mr. Sir stood over him and asked, "How does my face look to you now?"
A gurgling sound came out of the boy's mouth, then he managed to gasp the word, "Fine."
"I'm kind of handsome, don't you think?"
"Yes, Mr. Sir."

Out on the lake, the other boys asked Stanley what he knew about Mr. Sir's face, but he just shrugged and dug his hole. If he didn't talk about it, maybe it would go away.

He worked as hard and as fast as he could, not trying to pace himself. He just wanted to get off the lake and away from Mr. Sir as soon as possible. Besides, he knew he'd get a break.

"Whenever you're ready, just let me know," Zero had said.

The first time the water truck came, it was driven by Mr. Pendanski. The second time, Mr. Sir was driving.

No one said anything except "Thank you, Mr. Sir" as he filled each canteen. No one even dared to look at his grotesque face.

As Stanley waited, he ran his tongue over the roof of his mouth and inside his cheeks. His mouth was as dry and as parched as the lake. The bright sun reflected off the side mirror of the truck, and Stanley had to shield his eyes with his hand.

"Thank you, Mr. Sir," said Magnet, as he took his canteen from him.

"You thirsty, Caveman?" Mr. Sir asked.

"Yes, Mr. Sir," Stanley said, handing his canteen to him.

Mr. Sir opened the nozzle, and the water flowed out of the tank, but it did not go into Stanley's canteen. Instead, he held the canteen right next to the stream of water.

Stanley watched the water splatter on the dirt, where it was quickly absorbed by the thirsty ground.

Mr. Sir let the water run for about thirty seconds, then stopped. "You want more?" he asked.

Stanley didn't say anything.

Mr. Sir turned the water back on, and again Stanley watched it pour onto the dirt.

"There, that should be plenty" He handed Stanley his empty canteen.

Stanley stared at the dark spot on the ground, which quickly shrank before his eyes.

"Thank you, Mr. Sir," he said.

to pace oneself to control the speed that you move at so that you do not use up your energy too quickly

parched made dry, hot or thirsty

nozzle the narrow end-piece fitted to a pipe, hose, etc. to regulate the flow of liquid

25

There was a doctor in the town of Green Lake, one hundred and ten years ago. His name was Dr. Hawthorn. And whenever people got sick, they would go see Doc Hawthorn. But they would also see Sam, the onion man.

"Onions! Sweet, fresh onions!" Sam would call, as he and his donkey, Mary Lou, walked up and down the dirt roads of Green Lake. Mary Lou pulled a cart full of onions.

onion *Zwiebel*

batch a quantity of sth that is produced at the same time

at no charge for free

Sam's onion field was somewhere on the other side of the lake. Once or twice a week he would row across the lake and pick a new batch to fill the cart. Sam had big strong arms, but it would still take all day for him to row across the lake and another day for him to return. Most of the time he would leave Mary Lou in a shed, which the Walkers let him use at no charge, but sometimes he would take Mary Lou on his boat with him.

Sam claimed that Mary Lou was almost fifty years old, which was, and still is, extraordinarily old for a donkey.

"She eats nothing but raw onions," Sam would say, holding up a white onion between his dark fingers. "It's nature's magic vegetable. If a person ate nothing but raw onions, he could live to be two hundred years old."

Sam was not much older than twenty, so nobody was quite sure that Mary Lou was really as old as he said she was. How would he know?

to digest to change food that you have just eaten into substances that your body can use
digestible easy for the stomach to process
digestion the process of digesting food
digestive connected with the process of digestion; e. g. digestive biscuit

Still, nobody ever argued with Sam. And whenever they were sick, they would go not only to Doc Hawthorn but also to Sam.

Sam always gave the same advice: "Eat plenty of onions."

He said that onions were good for the digestion, the liver, the stomach, the lungs, the heart, and the brain. "If you don't believe me, just look at old Mary Lou here. She's never been sick a day in her life."

ointment a soft cream that you rub into your skin to heal or protect it
wart *Warze*
pimple *Pickel*
★ **remedy** a medicine that cures a disease or reduces its symptoms
to resent *übel nehmen*

He also had many different ointments, lotions, syrups, and pastes all made out of onion juice and different parts of the onion plant. This one cured asthma. That one was for warts and pimples. Another was a remedy for arthritis.

He even had a special ointment which he claimed would cure baldness. "Just rub it on your husband's head every night when he's sleeping, Mrs. Collingwood, and soon his hair will be as thick and as long as Mary Lou's tail."

Doc Hawthorn did not resent Sam. The folks of Green Lake were afraid to take chances. They would get regular medicine from Doc Hawthorn and onion concoctions from Sam. After they got over their illness, no one could be sure, not even Doc Hawthorn, which of the two treatments had done the trick.

concoction drink or food made by mixing different things, esp. in an unusual way
to do the trick *(colloq)* to bring about the desired result

Doc Hawthorn was almost completely bald, and in the morning his head often smelled like onions.

Whenever Katherine Barlow bought onions, she always bought an extra one or two and would let Mary Lou eat them out of her hand.

"Is something wrong?" Sam asked her one day as she was feeding Mary Lou. "You seem distracted."

distracted anxious, worried

"Oh, just the weather," said Miss Katherine. "It looks like rain clouds moving in."

"Me and Mary Lou, we like the rain," said Sam.

"Oh, I like it fine," said Miss Katherine, as she rubbed the donkey's rough hair on top of its head. "It's just that the roof leaks in the schoolhouse."

"I can fix that," said Sam.

"What are you going to do?" Katherine joked. "Fill the holes with onion paste?"

Sam laughed. "I'm good with my hands," he told her. "I built my own boat. If it leaked, I'd be in big trouble."

Katherine couldn't help but notice his strong, firm hands. They made a deal. He agreed to fix the leaky roof in exchange for six jars of spiced peaches.

It took Sam a week to fix the roof, because he could only work in the afternoons, after school let out and before night classes began. Sam wasn't allowed to attend classes because he was a Negro, but they let him fix the building.

Miss Katherine usually stayed in the schoolhouse, grading papers and such, while Sam worked on the roof. She enjoyed what little conversation they were able to have, shouting up and down to each other. She was surprised by his interest in poetry. When he took a break, she would sometimes read a poem to him. On more than one occasion, she would start to read a poem by Poe or Longfellow, only to hear him finish it for her, from memory.

She was sad when the roof was finished.

"Is something wrong?" he asked.

"No, you did a wonderful job," she said. "It's just that … the windows won't open. The children and I would enjoy a breeze now and then."

"I can fix that," said Sam.

She gave him two more jars of peaches and Sam fixed the windows.

It was easier to talk to him when he was working on the windows. He told her about his secret onion field on the other side of the lake, "where the onions grow all year round, and the water runs uphill."

When the windows were fixed, she complained that her desk wobbled.

"I can fix that," said Sam.

The next time she saw him, she mentioned that "the door doesn't hang straight," and she got to spend another afternoon with him while he fixed the door.

(Sam is not allowed to attend class.)
In 1876, **Jim Crow laws** were introduced that were the basis for segregation between blacks and whites in public schools, public transportation, etc.

to grade to give a mark to a piece of schoolwork

Edgar Allan Poe (1809–49) an American author, who is best known for his tales of mystery and the macabre, and who was also one of the first writers to make use of the short story genre.

Henry Wadsworth Longfellow (1807–82) an American poet and educator, who in his day was highly popular and well-known for his lyric poetry. Other famous works include *The Song of Hiawatha*, *Evangeline* and a translation of Dante's *The Divine Comedy*.

breeze a gentle wind

to wobble to move, rock or sway unsteadily from side to side

run-down in very bad condition

By the end of the first semester, Onion Sam had turned the old run-down schoolhouse into a well-crafted, freshly painted jewel of a building that the whole town was proud of. People passing by would stop and admire it. "That's our schoolhouse. It shows how much we value education here in Green Lake."

The only person who wasn't happy with it was Miss Katherine. She'd run out of things needing to be fixed.

She sat at her desk one afternoon, listening to the pitter-patter of the rain on the roof. No water leaked into the classroom, except for the few drops that came from her eyes.

"Onions! Hot sweet onions!" Sam called, out on the street.

She ran to him. She wanted to throw her arms around him but couldn't bring herself to do it. Instead she hugged Mary Lou's neck.

"Is something wrong?" he asked her.

"Oh, Sam," she said. "My heart is breaking."

"I can fix that," said Sam.

She turned to him.

He took hold of both of her hands, and kissed her.

Because of the rain, there was nobody else out on the street. Even if there was, Katherine and Sam wouldn't have noticed. They were lost in their own world.

At that moment, however, Hattie Parker stepped out of the general store. They didn't see her, but she saw them. She pointed her quivering finger in their direction and whispered, "God will punish you!"

general store shop in a small town that sells a wide variety of goods

to quiver to shake slightly

26

There were no telephones, but word spread quickly through the small town. By the end of the day, everyone in Green Lake had heard that the schoolteacher had kissed the onion picker.

Why are there no children at school? ➔

Not one child showed up for school the next morning.

Miss Katherine sat alone in the classroom and wondered if she had lost track of the day of the week. Perhaps it was Saturday. It wouldn't have surprised her.

to lose track of to fail to remember or notice sth

Her brain and heart had been spinning ever since Sam kissed her.

to spin to turn round and round quickly

She heard a noise outside the door, then suddenly a mob of men and women came storming into the school building. They were led by Trout Walker.

"There she is!" Trout shouted. "The Devil Woman!"

The mob was turning over desks and ripping down bulletin boards.

"She's been poisoning your children's brains with books," Trout declared.

They began piling all the books in the center of the room.

"Think about what you are doing!" cried Miss Katherine.

Someone made a grab for her, tearing her dress, but she managed to get out of the building. She ran to the sheriff's office.

The sheriff had his feet up on his desk and was drinking from a bottle of whiskey. "Mornin', Miss Katherine," he said.

"They're destroying the schoolhouse," she said, gasping for breath. "They'll burn it to the ground if someone doesn't stop them!"

"Just calm your pretty self down a second," the sheriff said in a slow drawl. "And tell me what you're talking about." He got up from his desk and walked over to her.

"Trout Walker has –"

"Now don't go saying nothing bad about Charles Walker," said the sheriff.

"We don't have much time!" urged Katherine. "You've got to stop them."

"You're sure pretty," said the sheriff.

Miss Katherine stared at him in horror.

"Kiss me," said the sheriff.

She slapped him across the face.

He laughed. "You kissed the onion picker. Why won't you kiss me?"

She tried to slap him again, but he caught her by the hand. She tried to wriggle free. "You're drunk!" she yelled.

"I always get drunk before a hanging."

"A hanging? Who –"

"It's against the law for a Negro to kiss a white woman."

"Well, then you'll have to hang me, too," said Katherine. "Because I kissed him back."

"It ain't against the law for you to kiss him," the sheriff explained. "Just for him to kiss you."

"We're all equal under the eyes of God," she declared.

The sheriff laughed. "Then if Sam and I are equal, why won't you kiss me?" He laughed again. "I'll make you a deal. One sweet kiss, and I won't hang your boyfriend. I'll just run him out of town."

mob a noisy and hostile group of people

to make a grab for to try to seize hold of

drawl *gedehnte Sprechweise*

to slap to hit sth or sb with the palm of your hand

to wriggle free to escape from sb's hold by making quick, small movements

(It is against the law.)
As late as 1967, all southern states still had laws that made marriage between black and white people illegal.

to run sb out of town to force sb to leave town by using violence

to jerk to move with a quick sudden movement

to hitch to tie, esp. temporarily

Miss Katherine jerked her hand free. As she hurried to the door, she heard the sheriff say, "The law will punish Sam. And God will punish you."

She stepped back into the street and saw smoke rising from the schoolhouse. She ran down to the lakefront, where Sam was hitching Mary Lou to the onion cart.

"Thank God, I found you," she sighed, hugging him. "We've got to get out of here. Now!"

"'What –"

"Someone must have seen us kissing yesterday," she said. "They set fire to the schoolhouse. The sheriff said he's going to hang you!"

Sam hesitated for a moment, as if he couldn't quite believe it. He didn't want to believe it. "C'mon, Mary Lou."

"We have to leave Mary Lou behind," said Katherine.

Sam stared at her a moment. There were tears in his eyes. "Okay."

Sam's boat was in the water, tied to a tree by a long rope. He untied it, and they waded through the water and climbed aboard. His powerful arms rowed them away from the shore. But his powerful arms were no match for Trout Walker's motorized boat. They were little more than halfway across the lake when Miss Katherine heard the loud roar of the engine. Then she saw the ugly black smoke ...

These are the facts:

The Walker boat smashed into Sam's boat. Sam was shot and killed in the water. Katherine Barlow was rescued against her wishes. When they returned to the shore, she saw Mary Lou's body lying on the ground.

The donkey had been shot in the head.

That all happened one hundred and ten years ago.

Since then, not one drop of rain has fallen on Green Lake.

You make the decision: Whom did God punish?

Three days after Sam's death, Miss Katherine shot the sheriff while he was sitting in his chair drinking a cup of coffee. Then she carefully applied a fresh coat of red lipstick and gave him the kiss he had asked for.

For the next twenty years Kissin' Kate Barlow was one of the most feared outlaws in all the West.

27

Stanley dug his shovel into the ground. His hole was about three and a half feet deep in the center. He grunted as he pried up some dirt, then flung it off to the side. The sun was almost directly overhead.

to grunt to make short low sounds

He glanced at his canteen lying beside his hole. He knew it was half full, but he didn't take a drink just yet. He had to drink sparingly, because he didn't know who would be driving the water truck the next time it came.

sparingly *sparsam*

Three days had passed since the Warden had scratched Mr. Sir. Every time Mr. Sir delivered water, he poured Stanley's straight onto the ground.

Fortunately, Mr. Pendanski delivered the water more often than Mr. Sir. Mr. Pendanski was obviously aware of what Mr. Sir was doing, because he always gave Stanley a little extra. He'd fill Stanley's canteen, then let Stanley take a long drink, then top it off for him.

to top off to fill to the top

It helped, too, that Zero was digging some of Stanley's hole for him. Although, as Stanley had expected, the other boys didn't like to see Stanley sitting around while they were working. They'd say things like "Who died and made you king?" or "It must be nice to have your own personal slave."

When he tried pointing out that he was the one who took the blame for the sunflower seeds, the other boys said it was his fault because he was the one who spilled them. "I risked my life for those seeds," Magnet had said, "and all I got was one lousy handful."

lousy *miserabel*

Stanley had also tried to explain that he needed to save his energy so he could teach Zero how to read, but the other boys just mocked him.

★ **to mock** to make fun of

"Same old story, ain't it, Armpit?" X-Ray had said.

"The white boy sits around while the black boy does all the work. Ain't that right, Caveman?"

"No, that's not right," Stanley replied.

"No, it ain't," X-Ray agreed. "It ain't right at all."

Stanley dug out another shovelful of dirt. He knew X-Ray wouldn't have been talking like that if *he* was the one teaching Zero to read. Then X-Ray would be talking about how important it was that he got his rest, *right*? So he could be a better teacher, *right*?

And that was true. He did need to save his strength so he could be a better teacher, although Zero was a quick learner.

Sometimes, in fact, Stanley hoped the Warden was watching them, with her secret cameras and microphones, so she'd know that Zero wasn't as stupid as everyone thought.

From across the lake he could see the approaching dust cloud. He took a drink from his canteen, then waited to see who was driving the truck.

* * *

The swelling on Mr. Sir's face had gone down, but it was still a little puffy. There had been three scratch marks down his cheek. Two of the marks had faded, but the middle scratch must have been the deepest, because it still remained. It was a jagged purple line running from below his eye to below his mouth, like a tattoo of a scar.

jagged having a rough edge

Stanley waited in line, then handed him his canteen.

Mr. Sir held it up to his ear and shook it. He smiled at the swishing sound.

Stanley hoped he wouldn't dump it out.

To his surprise, Mr. Sir held the canteen under the stream of water and filled it.

"Wait here," he said.

Still holding Stanley's canteen, Mr. Sir walked past him, then went around the side of the truck and into the cab, where he couldn't be seen.

cab part of the truck that the driver sits in

"What's he doing in there?" asked Zero.

"I wish I knew," said Stanley.

A short while later, Mr. Sir came out of the truck and handed Stanley his canteen. It was still full.

"Thank you, Mr. Sir."

Mr. Sir smiled at him. "What are you waiting for?" he asked. "Drink up." He popped some sunflower seeds into his mouth, chewed, and spit out the shells.

Stanley was afraid to drink it. He hated to think what kind of vile substance Mr. Sir might have put in it.

vile evil, disgusting

He brought the canteen back to his hole. For a long time, he left it beside his hole as he continued to dig. Then, when he was so thirsty that he could hardly stand it anymore, he unscrewed the cap, turned the canteen over, and poured it all out onto the dirt. He was afraid that if he'd waited another second, he might have taken a drink.

After Stanley taught Zero the final six letters of the alphabet, he taught him to write his name.

"Capital Z-e-r-o."

Zero wrote the letters as Stanley said them. "Zero," he said, looking at his piece of paper. His smile was too big for his face.

Stanley watched him write it over and over again.

Zero Zero Zero Zero Zero Zero Zero ...

In a way, it made him sad. He couldn't help but think that a hundred times zero was still nothing.

"You know, that's not my real name," Zero said as they headed to the Wreck Room for dinner.

"Well, yeah," Stanley said, "I guess I knew that." He had never really been sure.

"Everyone's always called me Zero, even before I came here.

"Oh. Okay."

"My real name is Hector."

"Hector," Stanley repeated.

"Hector Zeroni."

28

After twenty years, Kate Barlow returned to Green Lake. It was a place where nobody would ever find her – a ghost town on a ghost lake.

The peach trees had all died, but there were a couple of small oak trees still growing by an old abandoned cabin. The cabin used to be on the eastern shore of the lake. Now the edge of the lake was over five miles away, and it was little more than a small pond full of dirty water.

abandoned left empty by the people who owned it

She lived in the cabin. Sometimes she could hear Sam's voice echoing across the emptiness. "Onions! Sweet fresh onions."

She knew she was crazy. She knew she'd been crazy for the last twenty years.

"Oh, Sam," she would say, speaking into the vast emptiness. "I know it is hot, but I feel so very cold. My hands are cold. My feet are cold. My face is cold. My heart is cold."

* **vast** unusually large

And sometimes she would hear him say, "I can fix that," and she'd feel his warm arm across her shoulders.

She'd been living in the cabin about three months when she was awakened one morning by someone kicking open the cabin door. She opened her eyes to see the blurry end of a rifle, two inches from her nose.

blurry unable to be seen clearly; *verschwommen*
rifle a long gun which you hold up to your shoulder to shoot

loot goods or money that have been stolen
to yawn to open your mouth wide and breathe deeply because you are tired
to rummage to search for sth by moving things around in a frantic manner
blotchy marked with irregularly-shaped spots and red patches
scraggly untidy and uneven
to jab to stab or poke sharply
desperate *verzweifelt*
livestock animals, such as cows and sheep, that are kept on a farm to produce food or to be sold
★ **drought** long period of dry weather
turquoise a valuable greenish-blue stone or a jewel that is made from this
studded decorated with a lot of small jewels

She could smell Trout Walker's dirty feet.

"You've got exactly ten seconds to tell me where you've hidden your loot," said Trout. "Or else I'll blow your head off."

She yawned.

A redheaded woman was there with Trout. Kate could see her rummaging through the cabin, dumping drawers and knocking things from the shelves of cabinets.

The woman came to her. "Where is it?" she demanded.

"Linda Miller?" asked Kate. "Is that you?"

Linda Miller had been in the fourth grade when Kate Barlow was still a teacher. She had been a cute freckle-faced girl with beautiful red hair. Now her face was blotchy, and her hair was dirty and scraggly.

"It's Linda Walker now," said Trout.

"Oh, Linda, I'm so sorry," said Kate.

Trout jabbed her throat with the rifle. "Where's the loot?"

"There is no loot," said Kate.

"Don't give me that!" shouted Trout. "You've robbed every bank from here to Houston."

"You better tell him," said Linda. "We're desperate."

"You married him for his money, didn't you?" asked Kate.

Linda nodded. "But it's all gone. It dried up with the lake. The peach trees. The livestock. I kept thinking: It has to rain soon. The drought can't last forever. But it just kept getting hotter and hotter and hotter ..." Her eyes fixed on the shovel, which was leaning up against the fireplace. "She's buried it!" she declared.

"I don't know what you're talking about," said Kate.

There was a loud blast as Trout fired his rifle just above her head. The window behind her shattered. "Where's it buried?" he demanded.

"Go ahead and kill me, Trout," said Kate. "But I sure hope you like to dig. 'Cause you're going to be digging for a long time. It's a big vast wasteland out there. You, and your children, and their children, can dig for the next hundred years and you'll never find it."

Linda grabbed Kate's hair and jerked her head back. "Oh, we're not going to kill you," she said. "But by the time we're finished with you, you're going to wish you were dead."

"I've been wishing I was dead for the last twenty years," said Kate.

They dragged her out of bed and pushed her outside. She wore blue silk pajamas. Her turquoise-studded black boots remained beside her bed.

They loosely tied her legs together so she could walk, but she couldn't run. They made her walk barefoot on the hot ground.

They wouldn't let her stop walking.

"Not until you take us to the loot," said Trout.

Linda hit Kate on the back of her legs with the shovel. "You're going to take us to it sooner or later. So you might as well make it sooner."

She walked one way, then the other, until her feet were black and blistered. Whenever she stopped, Linda whacked her with the shovel.

"I'm losing my patience," warned Trout.

She felt the shovel jab into her back, and she fell onto hard dirt.

"Get up!" ordered Linda.

Kate struggled to her feet.

"We're being easy on you today," said Trout. "It's just going to keep getting worse and worse for you until you take us to it."

"Look out!" shouted Linda.

A lizard leaped toward them. Kate could see its big red eyes. Linda tried to hit it with the shovel, and Trout shot at it, but they both missed.

The lizard landed on Kate's bare ankle. Its sharp black teeth bit into her leg. Its white tongue lapped up the droplets of blood that leaked out of the wound.

Kate smiled. There was nothing they could do to her anymore. "Start digging," she said.

"Where is it?" Linda screeched.

"Where'd you bury it?" Trout demanded.

Kate Barlow died laughing.

blistered *blasig*
to whack to hit hard

ankle the joint connecting the foot and leg

to screech to scream in a high-pitched voice

PART TWO

THE LAST HOLE

29

humid *schwül*
drenched wet through and through, soaked
frizzy very tightly curled
★ **peak** the highest point
delirious mentally confused due to illness, shock, high fever, etc.

There was a change in the weather.

For the worse.

The air became unbearably humid. Stanley was drenched in sweat. Beads of moisture ran down the handle of his shovel. It was almost as if the temperature had gotten so hot that the air itself was sweating.

A loud boom of thunder echoed across the empty lake.

A storm was way off to the west, beyond the mountains. Stanley could count more than thirty seconds between the flash of lightning and the clap of thunder. That was how far away the storm was. Sound travels a great distance across a barren wasteland.

Usually, Stanley couldn't see the mountains at this time of day. The only time they were visible was just at sunup, before the air became hazy. Now, however, the sky was very dark off to the west, and every time the lightning flashed, the dark shape of the mountains would briefly appear.

"C'mon, rain!" shouted Armpit. "Blow this way!"

"Maybe it'll rain so hard it will fill up the whole lake," said Squid. "We can go swimming."

"Forty days and forty nights," said X-Ray. "Guess we better start building us an ark. Get two of each animal, right?"

"Right," said Zigzag. "Two rattlesnakes. Two scorpions. Two yellow-spotted lizards."

The humidity, or maybe the electricity in the air, had made Zigzag's head even more wild-looking. His frizzy blond hair stuck almost straight out.

The horizon lit up with a huge web of lightning. In that split second Stanley thought he saw an unusual rock formation on top of one of the mountain peaks. The peak looked to him exactly like a giant fist, with the thumb sticking straight up.

Then it was gone.

And Stanley wasn't sure whether he'd seen it or not.

"I found refuge on God's thumb."

That was what his great-grandfather had supposedly said after Kate Barlow had robbed him and left him stranded in the desert.

No one ever knew what he meant by that. He was delirious when he said it.

"But how could he live for three weeks without food or water?" Stanley had asked his father.

"I don't know. I wasn't there," replied his father. "I wasn't born yet. My father wasn't born yet. My grandmother, your great-grandmother, was a nurse in the hospital where they treated him. He'd always talked about how she'd dab his forehead with a cool wet cloth. He said that's why he fell in love with her. He thought she was an angel."

to dab to pat or tap gently

"A real angel?"

His father didn't know.

"What about after he got better? Did he ever say what he meant by God's thumb, or how he survived?"

"No. He just blamed his no-good-pig-stealing-father."

The storm moved off farther west, along with any hope of rain. But the image of the fist and thumb remained in Stanley's head. Although, instead of lightning flashing behind the thumb, in Stanley's mind, the lightning was coming out of the thumb, as if it were the thumb of God.

30

The next day was Zigzag's birthday. Or so he said. Zigzag lay in his cot as everyone headed outside. "I get to sleep in, because it's my birthday."

Then a little while later he cut into the breakfast line, just in front of Squid. Squid told him to go to the end of the line. "Hey, it's my birthday," Zigzag said, staying where he was.

"It's not your birthday," said Magnet, who was standing behind Squid.

"Is too," said Zigzag. "July 8."

Stanley was behind Magnet. He didn't know what day of the week it was, let alone the date. It could have been July 8, but how would Zigzag know?

let alone *geschweige denn*

He tried to figure out how long he'd been at Camp Green Lake, if indeed it was July 8. "I came here on May 24," he said aloud. "So that means I've been here ..."

to figure out to think about a problem until you find the answer

"Forty-six days," said Zero.

Stanley was still trying to remember how many days there were in May and June. He looked at Zero. He'd learned not to doubt him when it came to math.

to doubt sb to be not sure that sb is right about sth

Forty-six days. It felt more like a thousand. He didn't dig a hole that first day, and he hadn't dug one yet today. That meant he'd dug forty-four holes – if it really was July 8.

"Can I have an extra carton of juice?" Zigzag asked Mr. Sir. "It's my birthday."

To everyone's surprise, Mr. Sir gave it to him.

Stanley dug his shovel into the dirt. Hole number 45. "The forty-fifth hole is the hardest," he said to himself.

But that really wasn't true, and he knew it. He was a lot stronger than when he first arrived. His body had adjusted somewhat to the heat and harsh conditions.

to adjust to gradually change to adapt to a new situation

Mr. Sir was no longer depriving him of water. After having to get by on less water for a week or so, Stanley now felt like he had all the water he could want.

to deprive sb of sth to prevent sb from having sth that they want or need

Of course it helped that Zero dug some of his hole for him each day, but that wasn't as great as everyone thought it was. He always felt awkward while Zero was digging his hole, unsure of what to do with himself. Usually he stood around awhile, before sitting off by himself on the hard ground, with the sun beating down on him.

★ **awkward** not relaxed or comfortable

It was better than digging.

But not a lot better.

When the sun came up a couple of hours later, Stanley looked for "the thumb of God." The mountains were little more than dark shadows on the horizon.

He thought he could make out a spot where the top of one mountain seemed to jut upward, but it didn't seem very impressive. A short time later the mountains were no longer visible, hidden behind the glare of the sun, reflecting off the dirty air.

to make out to see with difficulty

to jut upward to stick out and up

It was possible, he realized, that he was somewhere near where Kate Barlow had robbed his great-grandfather. If that was really her lipstick tube he'd found, then she must have lived somewhere around here.

Zero took his turn before the lunch break. Stanley climbed out of his hole, and Zero climbed down into it.

"Hey, Caveman," said Zigzag. "You should get a whip. Then if your slave doesn't dig fast enough, you can crack it across his back."

whip long thin piece of leather attached to a handle used for punishing people or animals

"He's not my slave," said Stanley. "We have a deal, that's all."

"A good deal for you," said Zigzag.

"It was Zero's idea, not mine."

"Don't you know, Zig?" said X-Ray, coming over. "Caveman's doing Zero a big favor. Zero likes to dig holes."

"He sure is a nice guy to let Zero dig his hole for him," said Squid.

"Well, what about me?" asked Armpit. "I like to dig holes, too. Can I dig for you, Caveman, after Zero's finished?"

The other boys laughed.

"No, I want to," said Zigzag. "It's my birthday."

Stanley tried his best to ignore them.

Zigzag kept at it. "Come on, Caveman. Be a pal. Let me dig your hole."

Stanley smiled, as if it were all a big joke.

When Mr. Pendanski arrived with water and lunch, Zigzag offered Stanley his place in line. "Since you're so much better than me."

Stanley remained where he was. "I didn't say I was bet –"

"You're insulting him, Zig," said X-Ray. "Why should Caveman take your place, when he deserves to be at the very front? He's better than all of us. Aren't you, Caveman?"

"No," said Stanley.

"Sure you are," said X-Ray. "Now come to the front of the line where you belong."

"That's okay," said Stanley.

"No, it's not okay," said X-Ray. "Get up here."

Stanley hesitated, then moved to the front of the line.

"Well, this is a first," Mr. Pendanski said, coming around the side of the truck. He filled Stanley's canteen and handed him a sack lunch.

Stanley was glad to get away. He sat down between his hole and Zero's. He was glad that he'd be digging his own hole for the rest of the day. Maybe the other boys would leave him alone. Maybe he shouldn't let Zero dig his hole for him anymore. But he needed to save his energy to be a good teacher.

He bit into his sandwich, which contained some kind of meat-and-cheese mixture that came in a can. Just about everything at Green Lake came in a can. The supply truck came once a month.

He glanced up to see Zigzag and Squid walking toward him.

"I'll give you my cookie if you let me dig your hole," said Zigzag.

Squid laughed.

"Here, take my cookie," said Zigzag, holding it out for him.

"No, thanks," said Stanley.

"C'mon, take my cookie," said Zigzag, sticking it in his face.

"Leave me alone," said Stanley.

to do sb a favor *jdm einen Gefallen tun*

pal a friend

★ **insult** a remark or action that is unintentionally offensive or deliberately rude
to insult to offend sb by saying or doing sth unintentionally offensive or deliberately rude
to insult sb's intelligence to say sth that suggests that you think sb is stupid
insulting/insultingly offensive or rude

supply truck delivery truck bringing food, drink and other everyday necessities

"Please eat my cookie," said Zigzag, holding it under Stanley's nose.

Squid laughed.

Stanley pushed it away.

Zigzag pushed him back. "Don't push me!"

"I didn't ..." Stanley got to his feet. He looked around. Mr. Pendanski was filling Zero's canteen.

Zigzag pushed him again. "I said, 'Don't push me.'"

Stanley took a step backward, carefully avoiding Zero's hole.

Zigzag kept after him. He shoved Stanley and said, "Quit pushing!"

"Lay off," said Armpit, as he, Magnet, and X-Ray joined them.

"Why should he?" snapped X-Ray. "Caveman's bigger. He can take care of himself."

"I don't want any trouble," Stanley said.

Zigzag pushed him hard. "Eat my cookie," he said. Stanley was glad to see Mr. Pendanski coming toward them, along with Zero.

"Hi, Mom," said Armpit. "We were just fooling around."

"I saw what was going on," Mr. Pendanski said. He turned to Stanley. "Go ahead, Stanley," he said. "Hit him back. You're bigger."

Stanley stared at Mr. Pendanski in astonishment.

"Teach the bully a lesson," said Mr. Pendanski.

Zigzag hit Stanley on the shoulder with his open hand. "Teach me a lesson," he challenged.

Stanley made a feeble attempt to punch Zigzag, then he felt a flurry of fists against his head and neck. Zigzag had hold of his collar with one hand and was hitting him with the other. The collar ripped and Stanley fell backward onto the dirt.

"That's enough!" Mr. Pendanski yelled.

It wasn't enough for Zigzag. He jumped on top of Stanley.

"Stop!" shouted Mr. Pendanski.

The side of Stanley's face was pressed flat against the dirt. He tried to protect himself, but Zigzag's fists slammed off his arms and pounded his face into the ground.

All he could do was wait for it to be over.

Then, suddenly, Zigzag was off of him. Stanley managed to look up, and he saw that Zero had his arm around Zigzag's long neck.

Zigzag made a gagging sound, as he desperately tried to pry Zero's arm off of him.

"You're going to kill him!" shouted Mr. Pendanski.

Zero kept squeezing.

* **to fool around** *Quatsch machen*

feeble weak and unconvincing

flurry a lot of confused and agitated activity

* **to slam** to hit with a lot of force

to pry off to remove sth with great difficulty

Armpit charged into them, freeing Zigzag from Zero's choke hold. The three boys fell to the ground in different directions. Mr. Pendanski fired his pistol into the air.

choke hold *Würgegriff*

The other counselors came running from the office, the tents, or out on the lake. They had their guns drawn, but holstered them when they saw the trouble was over.

to holster to put a gun back into its leather holder

The Warden walked over from her cabin.

"There was a riot", Mr. Pendanski told her. "Zero almost strangled Ricky."

★ **riot** out-of-control situation in which a large crowd of people behave in a violent way

The Warden looked at Zigzag, who was still stretching and massaging his neck. Then she turned her attention to Stanley, who was obviously in the worst condition. "What happened to you?"

"Nothing. It wasn't a riot."

"Ziggy was beating up the Caveman," said Armpit.

"Then Zero started choking Zigzag, and I had to pull Zero off of Zigzag. It was all over before Mom fired his gun."

"They just got a little hot, that's all," said X-Ray. "You know how it is. In the sun all day. People get hot, right? But everything's cool now."

"I see," the Warden said. She turned to Zigzag. "What's the matter? Didn't you get a puppy for your birthday?"

puppy a baby dog

"Zig's just a little hot," said X-Ray. "Out in the sun all day. You know how it is. The blood starts to boil."

"Is that what happened, Zigzag?" asked the Warden.

"Yeah," said Zigzag. "Like X-Ray said. Working so hard in the hot sun, while Caveman just sits around doing nothing. My blood boiled."

"Excuse me?" said the Warden. "Caveman digs his holes, just like everyone else."

Zigzag shrugged. "Sometimes."

"Excuse me?"

"Zero's been digging part of Caveman's hole every day," said Squid.

The Warden looked from Squid to Stanley to Zero.

"I'm teaching him to read and write," said Stanley.

"It's sort of a trade. The hole still gets dug, so what does it matter who digs it?"

trade an exchange

"Excuse me?" said the Warden.

"Isn't it more important for him to learn to read?" Stanley asked. "Doesn't that build character more than digging holes?"

"That's his character," said the Warden. "What about your character?"

Stanley raised and lowered one shoulder.

The Warden turned to Zero. "Well, Zero, what have you learned so far?"

Zero said nothing.

"Have you just been digging Caveman's hole for nothing?" the Warden asked him.

"He likes to dig holes," said Mr. Pendanski.

"Tell me what you learned yesterday," said the Warden. "Surely you can remember that."

Zero said nothing.

Mr. Pendanski laughed. He picked up a shovel and said, "You might as well try to teach this shovel to read! It's got more brains than Zero."

"The 'at' sound," said Zero.

"The 'at' sound," repeated the Warden. "Well then, tell me, what does c-a-t spell?"

Zero glanced around uneasily.

Stanley knew he knew the answer. Zero just didn't like answering questions.

"Cat," Zero said.

Mr. Pendanski clapped his hands. "Bravo! Bravo! The boy's a genius!"

"F-a-t?" asked the Warden.

Zero thought a moment.

Stanley hadn't taught him the "f" sound yet.

"Eff," Zero whispered. "Eff-at. Fat."

"How about h-a-t?" asked the Warden.

Stanley hadn't taught him the "h" sound either.

Zero concentrated hard, then said, "Chat."

All the counselors laughed.

"He's a genius, all right!" said Mr. Pendanski. "He's so stupid, he doesn't even know he's stupid."

to have it in for sb
to be determined to harm or criticise sb

Stanley didn't know why Mr. Pendanski seemed to have it in for Zero. If Mr. Pendanski only thought about it, he'd realize it was very logical for Zero to think that the letter "h" made the "ch" sound.

"Okay, from now on, I don't want anyone digging anyone else's hole," said the Warden. "And no more reading lessons."

"I'm not digging another hole," said Zero.

"Good," said the Warden. She turned to Stanley. "You know why you're digging holes? Because it's good for you. It teaches you a lesson. If Zero digs your hole for you, then you're not learning your lesson, are you?"

"I guess not," Stanley mumbled, although he knew they weren't digging just to learn a lesson. She was looking for something, something that belonged to Kissin' Kate Barlow.

"Why can't I dig my own hole, but still teach Zero to read?" he asked. "What's wrong with that?"

"I'll tell you what's wrong with that," the Warden said. "It leads to trouble. Zero almost killed Zigzag."

"It causes him stress," said Mr. Pendanski. "I know you mean well, Stanley, but face it. Zero's too stupid to learn to read. That's what makes his blood boil. Not the hot sun."

"I'm not digging another hole," said Zero.

Mr. Pendanski handed him the shovel. "Here, take it, Zero. It's all you'll ever be good for."

Zero took the shovel.

Then he swung it like a baseball bat.

The metal blade smashed across Mr. Pendanski's face. His knees crumpled beneath him. He was unconscious before he hit the ground.

to crumple to collapse

The counselors all drew their guns.

Zero held the shovel out in front of him, as if he were going to try to bat away the bullets. "I hate digging holes," he said. Then he slowly backed away.

"Don't shoot him," said the Warden. "He can't go anywhere. The last thing we need is an investigation."

★ **investigation** an official, systematic attempt to dig deeper and find out the truth behind sth, such as a crime or accident
investigative journalism news reporting that tries to dig deeper and find out the truth behind news stories
investigator sb whose job it is to dig deeper and find out the truth behind things, e.g. a private investigator
investigative designed to find information or ascertain facts
investigatory relating to investigating sth

Zero kept backing up, out past the cluster of holes the boys had been digging, then farther and farther out onto the lake.

"He's going to have to come back for water," the Warden said.

Stanley noticed Zero's canteen lying on the ground near his hole.

A couple of the counselors helped Mr. Pendanski to his feet and into the truck.

Stanley looked out toward Zero, but he had disappeared into the haze.

The Warden ordered the counselors to take turns guarding the shower room and Wreck Room, all day and all night. They were not to let Zero drink any water. When he returned, he was to be brought directly to her.

She examined her fingernails and said, "It's almost time for me to paint my nails again."

Before she left, she told the six remaining members of Group D that she still expected seven holes.

31

Stanley angrily dug his shovel into the dirt. He was angry at everyone – Mr. Pendanski, the Warden, Zigzag, X-Ray, and his no-good-dirty-rotten-pig-stealing-great-great-grandfather. But mostly he was angry at himself.

He knew he never should have let Zero dig part of his hole for him. He still could have taught him to read. If Zero could dig all day and still have the strength to learn, then he should have been able to dig all day and still have the strength to teach.

What he should do, he thought, was go out after Zero.

But he didn't.

None of the others helped him dig Zero's hole, and he didn't expect them to. Zero had been helping him dig his hole. Now he had to dig Zero's.

He remained out on the lake, digging during the hottest part of the day, long after everyone else had gone in. He kept an eye out for Zero, but Zero didn't come back.

It would have been easy to go out after Zero. There was nobody to stop him. He kept thinking that's what he should do. Maybe they could climb to the top of Big Thumb.

If it wasn't too far away. And if it was really the same place where his great-grandfather found refuge. And if, after a hundred years or so, water was still there.

refuge protection from danger

entire whole

It didn't seem likely. Not when an entire lake had gone dry.

And even if they did find refuge on Big Thumb, he thought, they'd still have to come back here, eventually. Then they'd both have to face the Warden, and her rattlesnake fingers.

Instead, he came up with a better idea, although he didn't have it quite all figured out yet. He thought that maybe he could make a deal with the Warden. He'd tell her where he really found the gold tube if she wouldn't scratch Zero.

He wasn't sure how he'd make this deal without getting himself in deeper trouble. She might just say, Tell me where you found it or I'll scratch you, too. Plus, it would mean X-Ray would get in trouble, too. She'd probably scratch him up as well.

X-Ray would be out to get him for the next sixteen months.

He dug his shovel into the dirt.

spigot a tap, esp. on the outside of a building

By the next morning, Zero still hadn't returned. Stanley saw one of the counselors sitting guard by the water spigot outside the shower wall.

Mr. Pendanski had two black eyes and a bandage over his nose. "I always knew he was stupid," Stanley heard him say.

Stanley was required to dig only one hole the next day. As he dug, he kept a constant watchout for Zero, but never saw him. Once again he considered going out on the lake to look for him, but he began to realize that it was already too late.

His only hope was that Zero had found God's thumb on his own. It wasn't impossible. His great-grandfather had found it. For some reason his great-grandfather had felt the urge to climb to the top of that mountain. Maybe Zero would feel the same urge.

If it was the same mountain. If water was still there.

He tried to convince himself it wasn't impossible.

There had been a storm just a few days ago. Maybe Big Thumb was actually some kind of natural water tower that caught and stored the rain.

It wasn't impossible.

He returned to his tent to find the Warden, Mr. Sir, and Mr. Pendanski all waiting for him.

"Have you seen Zero?" the Warden asked him.

"No."

"No sign of him at all?"

"No."

"Do you have any idea where he went?"

"No."

"You know you're not doing him any favors if you're lying," said Mr. Sir. "He can't survive out there for more than a day or two."

"I don't know where he is."

All three stared at Stanley as if they were trying to figure out if be was telling the truth. Mr. Pendanski's face was so swollen, he could barely open his eyes. They were just slits.

"You sure he has no family?" the Warden asked Mr. Pendanski.

"He's a ward of the state," Mr. Pendanski told her. "He was living on the streets when he was arrested."

"Is there anyone who might ask questions? Some social worker who took an interest in him?"

"He had nobody," said Mr. Pendanski. "He was nobody."

The Warden thought a moment. "Okay, I want you to destroy all of his records."

Mr. Pendanski nodded.

"He was never here," said the Warden.

Mr. Sir nodded.

urge a strong wish or need
to resist the urge to do sth to overcome the desire to do sth that you strongly wish to do

ward of the state an adult or child whose guardianship is determined by a judge who appoints a government agency to oversee their affairs

record written account of sth

A.G. – Attorney General the chief law officer of a country or state and the head of its legal system

cross reference *Querverweis*

"Can you get into the state files from our computer?" she asked Mr. Pendanski. "I don't want anyone in the A.G.'s office to know he was here."

"I don't think I can erase him completely from all the state files," said Mr. Pendanski. "Too many crossreferences. But I can make it so it would be very difficult for anyone to ever find a record of him. Like I said, though, no one will ever look. No one cares about Hector Zeroni."

"Good," said the Warden.

32

twitch an uncontrolled, jerky motion

to fidget to keep moving your hands or feet

* **vacancy** a place that is not being used and is therefore free for sb else

to hot-wire to start a car without a key by using the wires of the ignition systemse

Two days later a new kid was assigned to Group D. His name was Brian, but X-Ray called him Twitch because he was always fidgeting. Twitch was assigned Zero's bed, and Zero's crate.

Vacancies don't last long at Camp Green Lake.

Twitch had been arrested for stealing a car. He claimed he could break into a car, disconnect the alarm, and hot-wire the engine, all in less than a minute.

"I never plan to, you know, steal one," he told them. "But sometimes, you know, I'll be walking past a real nice car, parked in a deserted area, and, you know, I'll just start twitching. If you think I twitch now, you should see me when I'm around a car. The next thing I know, I'm behind the wheel."

Stanley lay on his scratchy sheets. It occurred to him that his cot no longer smelled bad. He wondered if the smell had gone away, or if he had just gotten used to it.

"Hey, Caveman," said Twitch. "Do we really have to get up at 4:30?"

"You get used to it," Stanley told him. "It's the coolest part of the day."

He tried not to think about Zero. It was too late. Either he'd made it to Big Thumb, or ...

What worried him the most, however, wasn't that it was too late. What worried him the most, what really ate at his insides, was the fear that it *wasn't* too late.

What if Zero was still alive, desperately crawling across the dirt searching for water?

He tried to force the image out of his mind.

The next morning, out on the lake, Stanley listened as Mr. Sir told Twitch the requirement for his hole: "... as wide and as deep as your shovel."

Twitch fidgeted. His fingers drummed against the wooden shaft of his shovel, and his neck moved from side to side.

"You won't be twitching so much after digging all day," Mr. Sir told him. "You won't have the strength to wiggle your pinkie." He popped some sunflower seeds in his mouth, deftly chewed them, and spat out the shells. "This isn't a Girl Scout camp."

The water truck came shortly after sunrise. Stanley got in line behind Magnet, ahead of Twitch.

What if it's not too late?

He watched Mr. Sir fill X-Ray's canteen. The image of Zero crawling across the hot dry dirt remained in his head.

But what could he do about it? Even if Zero was somehow alive after more than four days, how would Stanley ever find him? It would take days. He'd need a car.

Or a pickup truck. A pickup truck with a tank of water in the back.

Stanley wondered if Mr. Sir had left the keys in the ignition.

He slowly backed away from the line, then circled over to the side of the truck. He looked through the window. The keys were there, dangling in the ignition.

Stanley felt his fingers start to twitch.

He took a deep breath to steady himself and tried to think clearly. He had never driven before.

But how hard could it be?

This is really crazy, he told himself. Whatever he did, he knew he'd have to do it quickly, before Mr. Sir noticed.

It's too late, he told himself. Zero couldn't have survived.

But what if it wasn't too late?

He took another deep breath. *Think about this*, he told himself, but there wasn't time to think. He flung open the door to the truck and climbed quickly inside.

"Hey!" shouted Mr. Sir.

He turned the key and stepped on the gas pedal. The engine revved.

The truck didn't move.

He pressed the pedal to the floor. The engine roared, but the truck was motionless.

Mr. Sir came running around the side of the truck. The door was still open.

"Put it in gear!" shouted Twitch.

⋆ **requirement** sth that must be done

to wiggle to move with small movements from side to side
pinkie the smallest finger of the hand

⋆ **to crawl** to move on your hands and knees like a baby

to dangle to hang loosely

to fling, flung, flung open to open using a lot of force

to rev to rapidly increase the speed of, esp. an engine

to roar here: to make a continuous loud noise

gear *Gang(schaltung)*

gear shift *Schaltknüppel*
lever stick
to lurch to move suddenly in an erratic way
to accelerate to increase speed
lopsided unequal or uneven
to sigh *seufzen*
sore hurting; in pain

The gear shift was on the floor next to the seat. Stanley pulled the lever back until the arrow pointed to the letter D, for Drive.

The truck lurched forward. Stanley jerked back against the seat and tightly gripped the wheel as the truck accelerated. His foot was pressed to the floor.

The truck went faster and faster across the dry lake bed. It bounced over a pile of dirt. Suddenly Stanley was slammed forward, then instantly backward as an airbag exploded in his face. He fell out of the open door and onto the ground.

He had driven straight into a hole.

He lay on the dirt staring at the truck, which stuck lopsided into the ground. He sighed. He couldn't blame his no-good-dirty-rotten-pig-stealing-great-great-grandfather this time. This time it was his own fault, one hundred percent. He had probably just done the stupidest thing he had ever done in his short and miserable life.

He managed to get to his feet. He was sore but didn't think he had broken any bones. He glanced back at Mr. Sir, who remained where he was, staring at Stanley.

He ran. His canteen was strapped around his neck. It banged against his chest as he ran, and every time it hit against him, it reminded him that it was empty, empty, empty.

33

He slowed to a walk. As far as he could tell, nobody was chasing him. He could hear voices coming from back by the truck but couldn't make out the words. Occasionally he'd hear the revving of the engine, but the truck wasn't going anywhere anytime soon.

He headed in what he thought was the direction of Big Thumb. He couldn't see it through the haze.

Walking helped calm him down and allowed him to think clearly. He doubted he could make it to Big Thumb, and with no water in his canteen, he didn't want to risk his life on the hope that he'd find refuge there. He'd have to return to camp. He knew that. But he was in no hurry. It would be better to return later, after everyone had a chance to calm down. And as long as he'd come this far, he might as well look for Zero.

He decided he would walk as long as he could, until he was too weak to go any farther, then he'd turn around and go back.

He smiled as he realized that wouldn't quite work. He would only go *halfway* – halfway as far as he thought he could go, so that he'd still have the strength to return. Then he'd have to make a deal with the Warden, tell her where he found Kate Barlow's lipstick tube, and beg for mercy.

He was surprised by how far out the holes extended. He couldn't even see the camp compound anymore, but he still kept passing holes. Just when he thought he'd passed the last hole, he'd come across another cluster of them, a little farther away.

Back at the compound, they had dug in a systematic order, row upon row, allowing space for the water truck. But out here there was no system. It was as if every once in a while, in a fit of frustration, the Warden would just pick a spot at random, and say, "What the hell, dig here." It was like trying to guess the winning numbers in a lottery.

Stanley found himself looking down into each hole he passed. He didn't admit to himself what he was looking for.

After more than an hour had gone by, he thought he had surely seen the last hole, but then off to the left he saw another cluster of them. He didn't actually see the holes. He saw the mounds of dirt that surrounded them.

He stepped over the mounds and looked into the first hole.

His heart stopped.

Down at the bottom was a family of yellow-spotted lizards. Their large red eyes looked up at him.

He leapt back over the mound and ran.

He didn't know if they were chasing after him. He thought he might have seen one leap out of the hole.

He ran until he couldn't run any farther, then collapsed. They hadn't come after him.

He sat there awhile and caught his breath. As he got back to his feet, he thought he noticed something on the ground, maybe fifty yards away. It didn't look like much, maybe just a big rock, but in a land of nothingness, any little thing seemed unusual.

He walked slowly toward it. The encounter with the lizards had made him very cautius.

It turned out to be an empty sack of sunflower seeds. He wondered if it was the same one Magnet had stolen from Mr. Sir, although that didn't seem likely.

He turned it inside out and found one seed stuck to the burlap.

Lunch.

to beg for mercy *um Gnade bitten*

compound an area that contains a group of buildings

at random without any definite plan or pattern

to leap, leapt, leapt to jump suddenly

encounter meeting

burlap *Sackleinen*

34

The sun was almost directly overhead. He figured he could walk for no more than another hour, maybe two, before he had to turn back.

It seemed pointless. He could see there was nothing ahead of him. Nothing but emptiness. He was hot, tired, hungry, and, most of all, thirsty. Maybe he should just turn around now. Maybe he'd already gone *halfway* and didn't know it.

Then, looking around, he saw a pool of water less than a hundred yards away from where he was standing. He closed his eyes and opened them to make sure he wasn't imagining it. The pool was still there.

He hurried toward it. The pool hurried away from him, moving as he moved, stopping when he stopped.

mirage *Fata Morgana*

There wasn't any water. It was a mirage caused by the shimmering waves of heat rising off the dry ground.

He kept walking. He still carried the empty sack of sunflower seeds. He didn't know if he might find something to put in it.

After a while he thought he could make out the shape of the mountains through the haze. At first he wasn't sure if this was another kind of mirage, but the farther he walked, the clearer they came into a view. Almost straight ahead of him, he could see what looked like a fist, with its thumb sticking up.

He didn't know how far away it was. Five miles? Fifty miles? One thing was certain. It was more than halfway.

He kept walking toward it, although he didn't know why. He knew he'd have to turn around before he got there. But every time he looked at it, it seemed to encourage him, giving him the thumbs-up sign.

As he continued walking, he became aware of a large object on the lake. He couldn't tell what it was, or even if it was natural or man-made. It looked a little like a fallen tree, although it didn't seem likely that a tree would grow here. More likely, it was a ridge of dirt or rocks.

ridge sth long and thin that is raised above the things around it

The object, whatever it was, was not on the way to Big Thumb but off to the right. He tried to decide whether to go to it or continue toward Big Thumb. Or maybe just turn around.

There was no point in heading toward Big Thumb, he decided. He would never make it. For all he knew it was like chasing the moon. But he could make it to the mysterious object.

He changed directions. He doubted it was anything, but the fact that there was *something* in the middle of all this *nothing* made it hard for him to pass up. He decided to make the object his halfway point, and he hoped he hadn't already gone too far.

He laughed to himself when he saw what it was. It was a boat – or part of a boat anyway. It struck him as funny to see a boat in the middle of this dry and barren wasteland. But after all, he realized, this was once a lake.
The boat lay upside down, half buried in the dirt.
Someone may have drowned here, he thought grimly – at the same spot where he could very well die of thirst.
The name of the boat had been painted on the back. The upside-down red letters were peeled and faded, but Stanley could still read the name: *Mary Lou*.
On one side of the boat there was a pile of dirt and then a tunnel leading down below the boat. The tunnel looked big enough for a good-sized animal to crawl through.
He heard a noise. Something stirred under the boat.
It was coming out.
"Hey!" Stanley shouted, hoping to scare it back inside. His mouth was very dry, and it was hard to shout very loudly.
"Hey," the thing answered weakly.
Then a dark hand and an orange sleeve reached up out of the tunnel.

★ **to drown** to die from being under water for too long
grim sinister, macabre

to stir to move slightly

35

Zero's face looked like a jack-o'-lantern that had been left out too many days past Halloween – half rotten, with sunken eyes and a drooping smile. "Is that water?" he asked. His voice was weak and raspy. His lips were so pale they were almost white, and his tongue seemed to flop around uselessly in his mouth as he spoke, as if it kept getting in the way.
"It's empty," said Stanley. He stared at Zero, not quite believing that he was real. "I tried to bring you the whole water truck, but," he smiled sheepishly, "I drove it into a hole. I can't believe you're …"
"Me neither," said Zero.
"C'mon, we got to get back to camp."

jack-o'-lantern *Halloween-Kürbis*
rotten *vergammelt*
to droop to hang down
raspy harsh and rough

sheepish embarrassed for having done sth wrong

sploosh invented word to describe the splashing of the mushy contents of the jar

to scatter to spread things out in a disorderly way

lid cover for the open part of a container

strained marked by excessive effort

Zero shook his head. "I'm not going back."

"You have to. We both have to."

"You want some sploosh?" Zero asked.

"What?"

Zero shaded his eyes with his forearm. "It's cooler under the boat," he said.

Stanley watched Zero crawl back through his hole. It was a miracle he was still alive, but Stanley knew he would have to get him back to camp soon, even if he had to carry him.

He crawled after him, and was just able to squeeze his body through the hole. He never would have fit when he first came to Camp Green Lake. He'd lost a lot of weight.

As he pulled himself through, his leg struck something sharp and hard. It was a shovel. For a second Stanley wondered how it got there, but then remembered that Zero had taken it with him after striking Mr. Pendanski.

It was cooler under the boat, which was half buried in the dirt. There were enough cracks and holes in the bottom of the boat, now the roof, to provide light and ventilation. He could see empty jars scattered about.

Zero held a jar in his hand and grunted as he tried to unscrew the lid.

"What is it?"

"Sploosh!" His voice was strained as he worked on the jar. "That's what I call it. They were buried under the boat."

He still couldn't get the lid off. "I found sixteen jars. Here, hand me the shovel."

Stanley didn't have a lot of room to move. He reached behind him, grabbed the wooden end of the shovel, and held it out to Zero, blade first.

"Sometimes you just have to ..." Zero said, then he hit the jar against the blade of the shovel, breaking the top of the jar clean off. He quickly brought the jar to his mouth and licked the sploosh off the jagged edges before it spilled.

"Careful," Stanley warned.

Zero picked up the cracked lid and licked the sploosh off that as well. Then he handed the broken jar to Stanley. "Drink some."

Stanley held it in his hand and stared at it a moment. He was afraid of the broken glass. He was also afraid of the sploosh. It looked like mud. Whatever it was, he realized, it must have been in the boat when the boat sank. That meant it was probably over a hundred years old. Who knew what kind of bacteria might be living in it?

"It's good," said Zero, encouraging him.

He wondered if Zero had heard of bacteria. He raised the jar to his mouth and carefully took a sip.

It was a warm, bubbly, mushy nectar, sweet and tangy. It felt like heaven as it flowed over his dry mouth and down his parched throat. He thought it might have been some kind of fruit at some time, perhaps peaches.

Zero smiled at him. "I told you it was good."

Stanley didn't want to drink too much, but it was too good to resist. They passed the jar back and forth until it was empty.

"How many are left?" he asked.

"None," said Zero.

Stanley's mouth dropped. "Now I have to take you back," he said.

"I'm not digging any more holes," said Zero.

"They won't make you dig," Stanley promised. "They'll probably send you to a hospital, like Barf Bag."

"Barf Bag stepped on a rattlesnake," said Zero.

Stanley remembered how he'd almost done the same. "I guess he didn't hear the rattle."

"He did it on purpose," said Zero.

"You think?"

"He took off his shoe and sock first."

Stanley shivered as he tried to imagine it.

"What's Mar-ya Luh-oh-oo?" asked Zero.

"What?"

Zero concentrated hard. "Mar ya, Luh oh oo."

"I have no idea."

"I'll show you," said Zero. He crawled back out from under the boat.

Stanley followed. Back outside, he had to shield his eyes from the brightness.

Zero walked around to the back of the boat and pointed to the upside-down letters. "Mm-ar-yuh. Luh-oh-oo."

Stanley smiled. "Mary Lou. It's the name of the boat."

"Mary Lou," Zero repeated, studying the letters. "I thought 'y' made the 'yuh' sound."

"It does," said Stanley. "But not when it's at the end of a word. Sometimes 'y' is a vowel and sometimes it's a consonant."

Zero suddenly groaned. He grabbed his stomach and bent over.

"Are you all right?"

Zero dropped to the ground. He lay on his side, with his knees pulled up to his chest. He continued to groan.

Stanley watched helplessly. He wondered if it was the sploosh.

He looked back toward Camp Green Lake.

to take a sip to drink a small amount of a liquid
tangy *würzig*

parched made dry, hot or thirsty

★ **to shield** to protect

to groan to make a long, deep sound because you are in pain, upset, or disappointed

At least he thought it was the direction of Camp Green Lake. He wasn't entirely sure.

Zero stopped moaning and his body slowly unbent.

"I'm taking you back," said Stanley.

Zero managed to sit up. He took several deep breaths.

"Look, I got a plan so you won't get in trouble," Stanley assured him. "Remember when I found the gold tube. Remember, I gave it to X-Ray, and the Warden went crazy making us dig where she thought X-Ray found it. I think if I tell the Warden where I really found it, I think she'll let us off."

to let sb off to choose not to punish sb

"I'm not going back," said Zero.

"You've got nowhere else to go," said Stanley.

Zero said nothing.

"You'll die out here," said Stanley.

"Then I'll die out here."

Stanley didn't know what to do. He had come to rescue Zero and instead drank the last of his sploosh. He looked off into the distance. "I want you to look at something."

"I'm not –"

"I just want you to look at that mountain up there. See the one that has something sticking up out of it?"

"Yeah, I think."

"What does it look like to you? Does it look like anything?"

Zero said nothing.

But as he studied the mountain, his right hand slowly formed into a fist. He raised his thumb. His eyes went from the mountain, to his hand, then back to the mountain.

36

They put four of the unbroken jars in the burlap sack, in case they might be able to use them. Stanley carried the sack. Zero held the shovel.

"I should warn you," Stanley said. "I'm not exactly the luckiest guy in the world."

Zero wasn't worried. "When you spend your whole life living in a hole," he said, "the only way you can go is up."

They gave each other the thumbs-up sign, then headed out.

It was the hottest part of the day. Stanley's empty-empty-empty canteen was still strapped around his neck. He thought back to the water truck, and wished he'd at least stopped and filled his canteen before running off.

***

They hadn't gone very far before Zero had another attack. He clutched his stomach as he let himself fall to the ground. Stanley could only wait for it to pass. The sploosh had saved Zero's life, but it was now destroying him from the inside. He wondered how long it would be before he, too, felt the effects. He looked at Big Thumb. It didn't seem any closer than when they first started out.

to clutch to grip or hold tightly and firmly

Zero took a deep breath and managed to sit up.

"Can you walk?" Stanley asked him.

"Just give me a second," Zero said. He took another breath, then, using the shovel, pulled himself back to his feet. He gave Stanley the thumbs-up sign and they continued.

Sometimes Stanley would try to go for a long while without looking at Big Thumb. He'd make a mental snapshot of how it looked, then wait maybe ten minutes before looking at it again, to see if it seemed closer.

a mental snapshot a picture in your mind

It never did. It was like chasing the moon.

And if they ever reached it, he realized, then they'd still have to climb it.

"I wonder who she was," said Zero.

"Who?"

"Mary Lou," said Zero.

Stanley smiled. "I guess she was once a real person on a real lake. It's hard to imagine."

"I bet she was pretty," said Zero. "Somebody must have loved her a lot, to name a boat after her."

"Yeah," said Stanley. "I bet she looked great in a bathing suit, sitting in the boat while her boyfriend rowed."

Zero used the shovel as a third leg. Two legs weren't enough to keep him up. "I got to stop and rest," he said after a while.

Stanley looked at Big Thumb. It still didn't look any closer. He was afraid if Zero stopped, he might never get started again. "We're almost there," he said.

How does Stanley feel when Zero becomes so weak?

He wondered which was closer: Camp Green Lake or Big Thumb?

"I really have to sit down."

"Just see if you can go a little –"

Zero collapsed. The shovel stayed up a fraction of a second longer, perfectly balanced on the tip of the blade, then it fell next to him.

blade the flat cutting part of a sword, knife, shovel, etc.

to flash here: to show quickly

to quit to stop an activity

★ **exhausted** extremely tired

to unscrew to take off or out by turning

★**to pretend** to behave as if sth is true, even though you know it is not, in order to deceive people or for fun
pretension the act of trying to appear or sound more important or clever than you are
pretentious attempting to impress by affecting greater importance or merit than is actually possessed

Zero knelt, bent over with his head on the ground. Stanley could hear a very low moaning sound coming from him. He looked at the shovel and couldn't help but think that he might need it to dig a grave. Zero's last hole.

And who will dig a grave for me? he thought.

But Zero did get up, once again flashing thumbs-up.

"Give me some words," he said weakly.

It took Stanley a few seconds to realize what he meant. Then he smiled and said, "R-u-n."

Zero sounded it out to himself. "Rr-un, run. Run."

"Good. F-u-n."

"Fffun."

The spelling seemed to help Zero. It gave him something to concentrate on besides his pain and weakness.

It distracted Stanley as well. The next time he looked up at Big Thumb, it really did seem closer.

They quit spelling words when it hurt too much to talk. Stanley's throat was dry. He was weak and exhausted, yet as bad as he felt, he knew that Zero felt ten times worse. As long as Zero could keep going, he could keep going, too.

It was possible, he thought, he hoped, that he didn't get any of the bad bacteria. Zero hadn't been able to unscrew the lid. Maybe the bad germs couldn't get in, either. Maybe the bacteria were only in the jars which opened easily, the ones he was now carrying in his sack.

What scared Stanley the most about dying wasn't his actual death. He figured he could handle the pain. It wouldn't be much worse than what he felt now. In fact, maybe at the moment of his death he would be too weak to feel pain. Death would be a relief. What worried him the most was the thought of his parents not knowing what happened to him, not knowing whether he was dead or alive. He hated to imagine what it would be like for his mother and father, day after day, month after month, not knowing, living on false hope. For him, at least, it would be over. For his parents, the pain would never end.

He wondered if the Warden would send out a search party to look for him. It didn't seem likely. She didn't send anyone to look for Zero. But no one cared about Zero. They simply destroyed his files.

But Stanley had a family. She couldn't pretend he was never there. He wondered what she would tell them. And when?

"What do you think's up there?" Zero asked.

Stanley looked to the top of Big Thumb. "Oh, probably an Italian restaurant," he said.

Zero managed to laugh.

"I think I'll get a pepperoni pizza and a large root beer," said Stanley.

"I want an ice cream sundae," said Zero. "With nuts and whipped cream, and bananas, and hot fudge."

The sun was almost directly in front of them. The thumb pointed up toward it.

They came to the end of the lake. Huge white stone cliffs rose up before them.

Unlike the eastern shore, where Camp Green Lake was situated, the western shore did not slope down gradually. It was as if they had been walking across the flat bottom of a giant frying pan, and now they had to somehow climb up out of it.

They could no longer see Big Thumb. The cliffs blocked their view. The cliffs also blocked out the sun.

Zero groaned and clutched his stomach, but he remained standing. "I'm all right," he whispered.

Stanley saw a rut, about a foot wide and six inches deep, running down a cliff. On either side of the rut were a series of ledges. "Let's try there," he said.

It looked to be about a fifty-foot climb, straight up.

Stanley still managed to hold the sack of jars in his left hand as he slowly moved up, from ledge to ledge, crisscrossing the rut. At times he had to use the side of the rut for support, in order to make it to the next ledge.

Zero stayed with him, somehow. His frail body trembled terribly as he climbed the stone wall.

Some of the ledges were wide enough to sit on. Others stuck out no more than a few inches – just enough for a quick step.

Stanley stopped about two-thirds of the way up, on a fairly wide ledge. Zero came up alongside him.

"You okay?" Stanley asked.

Zero gave the thumbs-up sign. Stanley did the same.

He looked above him. He wasn't sure how he'd get to the next ledge. It was three or four feet above his head, and he didn't see any footholds. He was afraid to look down.

"Give me a boost", said Zero. "Then I'll pull you up with the shovel."

"You won't be able to pull me up," said Stanley.

"Yes, I will," said Zero.

Stanley cupped his hands together, and Zero stepped on his interwoven fingers. He was able to lift Zero high enough for him to grab the protruding slab of rock. Stanley continued to help him from below as Zero pulled himself onto the ledge.

root beer *colaartiges, alkoholfreies Getränk aus verschiedenen Pflanzenwurzeln*
sundae *Eisbecher*
hot fudge *Karamellsauce*

shore the land along the edge of an ocean, sea, lake or river

frying pan a shallow, long-handled pan, used for frying food

rut here: a deep mark or hole

ledge a more or less flat shelf of rock sticking out from a cliff or slope

frail fragile, weak
* **to tremble** to shake uncontrollably

boost a push upward or ahead

to interweave, interwove, interwoven *sich ineinander schlingen*
to protrude to stick out

While Zero was getting himself situated up there, Stanley attached the sack to the shovel by poking a hole through the burlap. He held it up to Zero.

Zero first grabbed hold of the sack, then the shovel. He set the shovel so that half the blade was supported by the rock slab. The wooden shaft hung down toward Stanley. "Okay," he said.

Stanley doubted this would work. It was one thing for him to lift Zero, who was half his weight. It was quite another for Zero to try to pull him up.

Stanley grabbed hold of the shovel as he climbed up the rock wall, using the sides of the rut to help support him. His hands moved one over the other, up the shaft of the shovel.

shaft here: the long, wooden handle of the shovel

He felt Zero's hand clasp his wrist.

He let go of the shaft with one hand and grabbed the top of the ledge.

He gathered his strength and for a brief second seemed to defy gravity as he took a quick step up the wall and, with Zero's help, pulled himself the rest of the way over the ledge.

to defy gravity *gegen die Gesetze der Schwerkraft verstoßen*

He caught his breath. There was no way he could have done that a few months ago.

He noticed a large spot of blood on his wrist. It took him a moment to realize that it was Zero's blood.

wrist *Handgelenk*

Zero had deep gashes in both hands. He had held on to the metal blade of the shovel, keeping it in place, as Stanley climbed.

gash a deep wound

Zero brought his hands to his mouth and sucked up his blood.

One of the glass jars had broken in the sack. They decided to save the pieces. They might need to make a knife or something.

They rested briefly, then continued on up. It was a fairly easy climb the rest of the way.

When they reached flat ground, Stanley looked up to see the sun, a fiery ball balancing on top of Big Thumb. God was twirling a basketball.

fiery intensely hot
to twirl to cause to rotate rapidly

Soon they were walking in the long thin shadow of the thumb.

37

"We're almost there," said Stanley. He could see the base of the mountain.

Now that they really were *almost there*, it scared him. Big Thumb was his only hope. If there was no water, no refuge, then they'd have nothing, not even hope.

There was no exact place where the flat land stopped and the mountain began. The ground got steeper and steeper, and then there was no doubt that they were heading up the mountain.

Stanley could no longer see Big Thumb. The slope of the mountain was in the way.

It became too steep to go straight up. Instead they zigzagged back and forth, increasing their altitude by small increments every time they changed directions.

Patches of weeds dotted the mountainside. They walked from one patch to another, using the weeds as footholds. As they got higher, the weeds got thicker. Many had thorns, and they had to be careful walking through them.

Stanley would have liked to stop and rest, but he was afraid they'd never get started again. As long as Zero could keep going, he could keep going, too. Besides, he knew they didn't have much daylight left.

As the sky darkened, bugs began appearing above the weed patches. A swarm of gnats hovered around them, attracted by their sweat. Neither Stanley nor Zero had the strength to try to swat at them.

"How are you doing?" Stanley asked.

Zero pointed thumbs up. Then he said, "If a gnat lands on me, it will knock me over."

Stanley gave him some more words. "B-u-g-s," he spelled.

Zero concentrated hard, then said, "Boogs."

Stanley laughed.

A wide smile spread across Zero's sick and weary face as well. "Bugs," he said.

"Good," said Stanley. "Remember, it's a short 'u' if there's no 'e' at the end. "Okay, here's a hard one. How about, l-u-n-c-h?"

"Luh – Luh-un –" Suddenly, Zero made a horrible, wrenching noise as he doubled over and grabbed his stomach. His frail body shook violently, and he threw up, emptying his stomach of the sploosh.

He leaned on his knees and took several deep breaths. Then he straightened up and continued going.

* **refuge** a place that provides shelter or protection

altitude height above ground level
increment *Stufe*
weed an unwanted plant growing wild
to dot to cover here and there like little spots
thorn a sharp point that grows along the stem of a plant to protect it

to swat to hit at with your hand

gnat *Stechmücke*

bug *Wanze*

weary physically or mentally exhausted
weariness extreme tiredness
to weary to cause to become extremely tired

to wrench to twist or turn suddenly
to double over here: to bend over in pain

The swarm of gnats stayed behind, preferring the contents of Zero's stomach to the sweat on the boys' faces.

Stanley didn't give him any more words, thinking that he needed to save his strength. But about ten or fifteen minutes later, Zero said, "Lunch."

As they climbed higher, the patches of weeds grew thicker, and they had to be careful not to get their feet tangled in thorny vines. Stanley suddenly realized something. There hadn't been any weeds on the lake.

to tangle *sich verheddern*

vine a climbing plant with thin stems; *Kletterplanze*

"Weeds and bugs," he said. "There's got to be water around somewhere. We must be getting close."

A wide clown-like smile spread across Zero's face. He flashed the thumbs-up sign, then fell.

He didn't get up. Stanley bent over him. "C'mon, Zero," he urged. "We're getting close. C'mon, Hector. Weeds and bugs. Weeds and boogs."

C'mon Come on

Stanley shook him. "I've already ordered your hot fudge sundae," he said. "They're making it right now."

Zero said nothing.

38

Stanley took hold of Zero's forearms and pulled him upright. Then he stooped down and let Zero fall over his right shoulder. He stood up, lifting Zero's worn-out body off the ground.

He left the shovel and sack of jars behind as he continued up the mountain. Zero's legs dangled in front of him.

Stanley couldn't see his feet, which made it difficult to walk through the tangled patches of weeds and vines. He concentrated on one step at a time, carefully raising and setting down each foot. He thought only about each step, and not the impossible task that lay before him.

Higher and higher he climbed. His strength came from somewhere deep inside himself and also seemed to come from the outside as well. After focusing on Big Thumb for so long, it was as if the rock had absorbed his energy and now acted like a kind of giant magnet pulling him toward it.

***to absorb** 1. to suck up or drink in 2. to grab your full attention
absorption 1. the process by which one thing absorbs or is absorbed by another 2. great mental concentration
absorptive having power or capacity to soak up something
absorbing grabbing your full attention

After a while he became aware of a foul odor. At first he thought it came from Zero, but it seemed to be in the air, hanging heavy all around him.

odor a smell, esp. an unpleasant one

He also noticed that the ground wasn't as steep anymore. As the ground flattened, a huge stone precipice rose up ahead of him, just barely visible in the moonlight. It seemed to grow bigger with each step he took.

It no longer resembled a thumb.

And he knew he'd never be able to climb it.

Around him, the smell became stronger. It was the bitter smell of despair.

Even if he could somehow climb Big Thumb, he knew he wouldn't find water. How could there be water at the top of a giant rock? The weeds and bugs survived only by an occasional rainstorm, like the one he had seen from camp.

Still, he continued toward it. If nothing else, he wanted to at least reach the Thumb.

He never made it.

His feet slipped out from under him. Zero's head knocked against the back of his shoulder as he fell and tumbled into a small muddy gully.

As he lay face down in the muddy ditch, he didn't know if he'd ever get up again. He didn't know if he'd even try. Had he come all this way just to ... *You need water to make mud!*

He crawled along the gully in the direction that seemed the muddiest. The ground became gloppier. The mud splashed up as he slapped the ground.

Using both hands, he dug a hole in the soggy soil. It was too dark to see, but he thought he could feel a tiny pool of water at the bottom of his hole. He stuck his head in the hole and licked the dirt.

He dug deeper, and as he did so, more water seemed to fill the hole. He couldn't see it, but he could feel it – first with his fingers, then with his tongue.

He dug until he had a hole that was about as deep as his arm was long. There was enough water for him to scoop out with his hands and drop on Zero's face.

Zero's eyes remained closed. But his tongue poked out between his lips, searching out the droplets.

Stanley dragged Zero closer to the hole. He dug, then scooped some more water and let it pour out of his hands into Zero's mouth.

As he continued to widen his hole, his hand came across a smooth, round object. It was too smooth and too round to be a rock.

He wiped the dirt off of it and realized it was an onion.

He bit into it without peeling it. The hot bitter juice burst into his mouth. He could feel it all the way up to his eyes.

precipice an extremely steep mass of rock or cliff face
★ **visible** able to be seen
★ **to resemble** to look like
★ **despair** hopelessness
to tumble to fall suddenly and sharply
gully deep ditch cut by water
Describe the effects of the discovery Stanley makes.
gloppy messy and sticky
soggy very wet and heavy
to scoop out *herausschöpfen*
to poke out to reach out, extend

And when he swallowed, he felt its warmth move down his throat and into his stomach.

He only ate half. He gave the other half to Zero.

"Here, eat this."

"What is it?" Zero whispered.

"A hot fudge sundae."

39

Stanley awoke in a meadow, looking up at the giant rock tower. It was layered and streaked with different shades of red, burnt orange, brown, and tan. It must have been over a hundred feet tall.

to streak to cover with a long, thin line, mark or trace of a different colour

Stanley lay awhile, just looking at it. He didn't have the strength to get up. It felt like the insides of his mouth and throat were coated with sand.

And no wonder. When he rolled over he saw the water hole. It was about two and a half feet deep and over three feet wide. At the bottom lay no more than two inches of very brown water.

two and half/three feet about 76 cm/91 cm

His hands and fingers were sore from digging, especially under his fingernails. He scooped some dirty water into his mouth, then swished it around, trying to filter it with his teeth.

to swish to move around with a hissing or rushing sound

Zero moaned.

Stanley started to say something to him, but no words came out of his mouth, and he had to try again. "How you doing?" It hurt to talk.

"Not good," Zero said quietly. With great effort, he rolled over, raised himself to his knees, and crawled to the water hole. He lowered his head into it and lapped up some water. Then he jerked back, clutched his knees to his chest, and rolled to his side. His body shook violently.

to lap up to take in food or liquid with your tongue

*__violent__ aggressively strong and powerful
violence the exercise or an instance of aggressive physical force
to violate to break or disregard a law or promise
violation the breaking or disregarding of a law or promise

Stanley thought about going back down the mountain to look for the shovel, so he could make the water hole deeper. Maybe that would give them cleaner water. They could use the jars as drinking glasses.

But he didn't think he had the strength to go down, let alone make it back up again. And he didn't know where to look.

He struggled to his feet. He was in a field of greenish white flowers that seemed to extend all the way around Big Thumb.

He took a deep breath, then walked the last fifty yards to the giant precipice and touched it.

Tag, you're it.

Then he walked back to Zero and the water hole. On the way he picked one of the flowers. It actually wasn't one big flower, he discovered, but instead each flower was really a cluster of tiny little flowers that formed a round ball. He brought it to his mouth but had to spit it out.

He could see part of the trail he had made the night before, when he carried Zero up the mountain. If he was going to head back down and look for the shovel, he realized, he should do it soon, while the trail was fresh. But he didn't want to leave Zero. He was afraid Zero might die while he was gone.

Zero was still lying doubled over on his side. "I got to tell you something," he said with a groan.

"Don't talk," said Stanley. "Save your strength."

"No, listen," Zero insisted, then he closed his eyes as his face twisted with pain.

"I'm listening," Stanley whispered.

"I took your shoes," Zero said.

Stanley didn't know what he was talking about. His shoes were on his feet. "That's all right," he said. "Just rest now."

"It's all my fault," said Zero.

"It's nobody's fault," said Stanley.

"I didn't know," Zero said.

"That's okay," Stanley said. "Just rest."

Zero closed his eyes. But then again he said, "I didn't know about the shoes."

"What shoes?"

"From the shelter."

It took a moment for Stanley to comprehend. "Clyde Livingston's shoes?"

"I'm sorry", said Zero.

Stanley stared at him. It was impossible. Zero was delirious.

Zero's "confession" seemed to bring him some relief. The muscles in his face relaxed. As he drifted into sleep, Stanley softly sang him the song that had been in his family for generations.

"If only, if only," the woodpecker sighs,
"The bark on the tree was just a little bit softer."
While the wolf waits below, hungry and lonely,
He cries to the moo-oo-oon,
"If only, if only."

"Tag, you're it." *beim Fangen spielen: "Du bist."*

★ **to discover** to become aware of a fact or situation

to twist to form into a bent and distorted shape

(homeless) shelter a place where people who have no home can live for free

delirious mentally confused due to illness, shock, high fever, etc.
confession admission that you did something wrong
woodpecker *Specht*
bark *Baumrinde*

40

★grateful thankful
gratitude a feeling of thankfulness or appreciation
to owe sb a debt of gratitude to be very thankful to sb for sth good that they have done for you that you can never repay

When Stanley found the onion the night before, he didn't question how it had come to be there. He ate it gratefully. But now as he sat gazing at Big Thumb and the meadow full of flowers, he couldn't help but wonder about it.

If there was one wild onion, there could be more.

He intertwined his fingers and tried to rub out the pain. Then he bent down and dug up another flower, this time pulling up the entire plant, including the root.

What is the function of the little "story in the story"?

to gaze at to look at sb or sth for a long time, often without realizing it, to stare
cart *Karre*

"Onions! Fresh, hot, sweet onions," Sam called as Mary Lou pulled the cart down Main Street. "Eight cents a dozen."

It was a beautiful spring morning. The sky was painted pale blue and pink – the same color as the lake and the peach trees along its shore.

nightgown a loose garment worn in bed by women and girls

Mrs. Gladys Tennyson was wearing just her nightgown and robe as she came running down the street after Sam. Mrs. Tennyson was normally a very proper woman who never went out in public without dressing up in fine clothes and a hat. So it was quite surprising to the people of Green Lake to see her running past them.

"Sam!" she shouted.

mule *Maultier*

"Whoa, Mary Lou," said Sam, stopping his mule and cart. "G'morning, Mrs. Tennyson," he said. "How's little Becca doing?"

Gladys Tennyson was all smiles. "I think she's going to be all right. The fever broke about an hour ago. Thanks to you."

"I'm sure the good Lord and Doc Hawthorn deserve most of the credit."

quack an unqualified person who pretends to be a doctor, but gives bad advice; a charlatan
leech *Blutegel*

"The Good Lord, yes," agreed Mrs. Tennyson, "but not Dr. Hawthorn. That quack wanted to put leeches on her stomach! Leeches! My word! He said they would suck out the bad blood. Now you tell me. How would a leech know good blood from bad blood?"

"I wouldn't know," said Sam.

"It was your onion tonic," said Mrs. Tennyson. "That's what saved her."

Other townspeople made their way to the cart. "Good morning, Gladys," said Hattie Parker. "Don't you look lovely this morning."

to snicker to laugh in a sly or disrespectful way

Several people snickered.

"Good morning, Hattie," Mrs. Tennyson replied.

"Does your husband know you're parading about in your bed clothes?" Hattie asked.

There were more snickers.

"My husband knows exactly where I am and how I am dressed, thank you," said Mrs. Tennyson. "We have both been up all night and half the morning with Rebecca. She almost died from stomach sickness. It seems she ate some bad meat."

Hattie's face flushed. Her husband, Jim Parker, was the butcher.

"It made my husband and me sick as well," said Mrs. Tennyson, "but it nearly killed Becca, what with her being so young. Sam saved her life."

"It wasn't me," said Sam. "It was the onions."

"I'm glad Becca's all right," Hattie said contritely.

"I keep telling Jim he needs to wash his knives," said Mr. Pike, who owned the general store.

Hattie Parker excused herself, then turned and quickly walked away.

"Tell Becca that when she feels up to it to come by the store for a piece of candy," said Mr. Pike.

"Thank you, I'll do that."

Before returning home, Mrs. Tennyson bought a dozen onions from Sam. She gave him a dime and told him to keep the change.

"I don't take charity," Sam told her. "But if you want to buy a few extra onions for Mary Lou, I'm sure she'd appreciate it."

"All right then," said Mrs. Tennyson, "give me my change in onions."

Sam gave Mrs. Tennyson an additional three onions, and she fed them one at a time to Mary Lou. She laughed as the old donkey ate them out of her hand.

Stanley and Zero slept off and on for the next two days, ate onions, all they wanted, and splashed dirty water into their mouths. In the late afternoon Big Thumb gave them shade. Stanley tried to make the hole deeper, but he really needed the shovel. His efforts just seemed to stir up the mud and make the water dirtier.

Zero was sleeping. He was still very sick and weak, but the sleep and the onions seemed to be doing him some good. Stanley was no longer afraid that he would die soon. Still, he didn't want to go for the shovel while Zero was asleep. He didn't want him to wake up and think he'd been deserted.

He waited for Zero to open his eyes.

"I think I'll go look for the shovel," Stanley said.

to parade to walk about in public in a way that attracts attention

to flush to redden, esp. from embarrassment or shame
butcher *Metzger*

contrite truly sorry

to feel up to sth to have enough energy to do sth

dime *Zehncentstück*

to take charity *Almosen annehmen*

to stir up to move around, esp. briskly

***to desert** to abandon
desertion the act of withdrawing support or help despite allegiance or responsibility

feebly weakly

"I'll wait here," Zero said feebly, as if he had any other choice.

Stanley headed down the mountain. The sleep and the onions had done him a lot of good as well. He felt strong.

It was fairly easy to follow the trail he had made two days earlier. There were a few places where he wasn't sure he was going the right way, but it just took a little bit of searching before he found the trail again.

He went quite a ways down the mountain but still didn't find the shovel. He looked back up toward the top of the mountain. He must have walked right past it, he thought. There was no way he could have carried Zero all the way up from here.

bare without any covering

Still, he headed downward, just in case. He came to a bare spot between two large patches of weeds and sat down to rest. Now he had definitely gone too far, he decided. He was tired out from walking *down* the hill. It would have been impossible to have carried Zero *up* the hill from here, especially after walking all day with no food or water. The shovel must be buried in some weeds.

indentation a cut, notch, or deep hole

Before starting back up, he took one last look around in all directions. He saw a large indentation in the weeds a little farther down the mountain. It didn't seem likely that the shovel could be there, but he'd already come this far.

There, lying in some tall weeds, he found the shovel and the sack of jars. He was amazed. He wondered if the shovel and sack might have rolled down the hill. But none of the jars were broken, except the one which had broken earlier. And if they had rolled down the hill, it is doubtful that he would have found the sack and shovel side by side.

On his way back up the mountain, Stanley had to sit down and rest several times. It was a long, hard climb.

41

improve to become better

Zero's condition continued to improve.

Stanley slowly peeled an onion. He liked eating them one layer at a time.

murky dark or dirty and difficult to see through

The water hole was now almost as large as the holes he had dug back at Camp Green Lake. It contained almost two feet of murky water. Stanley had dug it all himself. Zero had offered to help, but Stanley thought it better for Zero to save his strength. It was a lot harder to dig in water than it was in a dry lake.

Stanley was surprised that he himself hadn't gotten sick – either from the sploosh, the dirty water, or from living on onions. He used to get sick quite a lot back at home.

Both boys were barefoot. They had washed their socks. All their clothes were very dirty, but their socks were definitely the worst.

They didn't dip their socks into the hole, afraid to contaminate the water. Instead they filled the jars and poured the water over their dirty socks.

"I didn't go to the homeless shelter very often," Zero said. "Just if the weather was really bad. I'd have to find someone to pretend to be my mom. If I'd just gone by myself, they would have asked me a bunch of questions. If they'd found out I didn't have a mom, they would have made me a ward of the state."

"What's a ward of the state?"

Zero smiled. "I don't know. But I didn't like the sound of it."

Stanley remembered Mr. Pendanski telling the Warden that Zero was a ward of the state. He wondered if Zero knew he'd become one.

"I liked sleeping outside," said Zero. "I used to pretend I was a Cub Scout. I always wanted to be a Cub Scout. I'd see them at the park in their blue uniforms."

"I was never a Cub Scout," said Stanley. "I wasn't good at social stuff like that. Kids made fun of me because I was fat."

"I liked the blue uniforms," said Zero. "Maybe I wouldn't have liked being a Cub Scout."

Stanley shrugged one shoulder.

"My mother was once a Girl Scout", said Zero.

"I thought you said you didn't have a mother."

"Everybody has to have a mother."

"Well, yeah, I know that."

"She said she once won a prize for selling the most Girl Scout cookies," said Zero. "She was real proud of that."

Stanley peeled off another layer of his onion.

"We always took what we needed," Zero said. "When I was little, I didn't even know it was *stealing*. I don't remember when I found out. But we just took what we needed, never more. So when I saw the shoes on display in the shelter, I just reached in the glass case and took them."

"Clyde Livingston's shoes?" asked Stanley.

"I didn't know they were his. I just thought they were somebody's old shoes. It was better to take someone's old shoes, I

barefoot without shoes or socks

***to contaminate** to make sth impure and dirty
contamination the act or process of making sth impure

ward a person, esp. a child, who is under the legal protection of a court of law or another person

Cub Scout a member of the junior division of the Boy Scouts

thought, than steal a pair of new ones. I didn't know they were famous. There was a sign, but of course I couldn't read it. Then, the next thing I know everybody's making this big deal about how the shoes are missing. It was kind of funny, in a way. The whole place is going crazy. There I was, wearing the shoes, and everyone's running around saying, 'What happened to the shoes?' 'The shoes are gone!' I just walked out the door. No one noticed me. When I got outside, I ran around the corner and immediately took off the shoes. I put them on top of a parked car. I remember they smelled really bad."

to make a big deal about sth *viel Wind um etw machen*

"Yeah, those were them," said Stanley. "Did they fit you?"

"Pretty much."

Stanley remembered being surprised at Clyde Livingston's small shoe size. Stanley's shoes were bigger. Clyde Livingston had small, quick feet. Stanley's feet were big and slow.

"I should have just kept them," said Zero. "I'd already made it out of the shelter and everything. I ended up getting arrested the next day when I tried to walk out of a shoe store with a new pair of sneakers. If I had just kept those old smelly sneakers, then neither of us would be here right now."

* **sneakers** canvas shoes with rubber soles, typically worn for sports

42

Zero became strong enough to help dig the hole. When he finished, it was over six feet deep. He filled the bottom with rocks to help separate the water from the dirt.

He was still the best hole digger around.

"That's the last hole I will ever dig," he declared, throwing down the shovel.

to declare to announce with great ceremony

Stanley smiled. He wished it were true, but he knew they had no choice but to eventually return to Camp Green Lake. They couldn't live on onions forever.

eventually *letztendlich*

They had been completely around Big Thumb. It was like a giant sundial. They followed the shade.

sundial an instrument that indicates the time of day by shadows cast by the sun on its surface

They were able to see out in all directions. There was no place to go. The mountain was surrounded by desert.

Zero stared at Big Thumb. "It must have a hole in it," he said, "filled with water."

"You think?"

"Where else could the water be coming from?" Zero asked. "Water doesn't run uphill."

Stanley bit into an onion. It didn't burn his eyes or nose, and, in fact, he no longer noticed a particularly strong taste.

He remembered when he had first carried Zero up the hill, how the air had smelled bitter. It was the smell of thousands of onions, growing and rotting and sprouting.

Now he didn't smell a thing.

"How many onions do you think we've eaten?" he asked.

Zero shrugged. "I don't even know how long we've been here."

"I'd say about a week," said Stanley. "And we probably each eat about twenty onions a day, so that's …"

"Two hundred and eighty onions," said Zero.

Stanley smiled. "I bet we really stink."

Two nights later, Stanley lay awake staring up at the star-filled sky. He was too happy to fall asleep.

He knew he had no reason to be happy. He had heard or read somewhere that right before a person freezes to death, he suddenly feels nice and warm. He wondered if perhaps he was experiencing something like that.

It occurred to him that he couldn't remember the last time he felt happiness. It wasn't just being sent to Camp Green Lake that had made his life miserable. Before that he'd been unhappy at school, where he had no friends, and bullies like Derrick Dunne picked on him. No one liked him, and the truth was, he didn't especially like himself.

He liked himself now.

He wondered if he was delirious.

He looked over at Zero sleeping near him. Zero's face was lit in the starlight, and there was a flower petal in front of his nose that moved back and forth as he breathed. It reminded Stanley of something out of a cartoon. Zero breathed in, and the petal was drawn up almost touching his nose. Zero breathed out, and the petal moved toward his chin. It stayed on Zero's face for an amazingly long time before fluttering off to the side.

Stanley considered placing it back in front of Zero's nose, but it wouldn't be the same.

It seemed like Zero had lived at Camp Green Lake forever, but as Stanley thought about it now, he realized that Zero must have gotten there no more than a month or two before him.

Zero was actually arrested a day later. But Stanley's trial kept getting delayed because of baseball.

He remembered what Zero had said a few days before. If Zero had just kept those shoes, then neither of them would be here right now.

to sprout to begin to grow or develop

Describe the feelings and thoughts that cross Stanley's mind when he is lying awake at night.

to freeze to death to die due from being exposed to extreme cold for too long

★ **to occur to sb** *jdm einfallen*

★**miserable** unhappy or depressed

misery wretchedness of condition or circumstances

to put sb out of their misery to end a suspenseful or worrying situation or kill sb or sth as an act of mercy

bully sb who hurts, persecutes or intimidates weaker people

flower petal *Blütenblatt*

to flutter off *wegflattern*

trial a legal process in which a judge, and often also a jury, examine information to decide whether sb is guilty of a crime or not

to delay to wait until a later time to do sth

to glitter *glitzern*

★ **destiny** the things that will happen to sb in the future, esp. those that cannot be changed or controlled; fate

★**coincidence** a remarkable concurrence of events or circumstances without apparent causal connection
to coincide with something to agree with or match sth
by coincidence by an accidental and strange concurrence of events or circumstances

to sneak, snuck, snuck to go quietly and secretly
buzzard a type of large bird that eats dead animals
fugitive sb who has escaped from prison and is hiding from the law

★ **to bother** to take the trouble to do sth

to pop into one's head to suddenly think of sth

treasure chest *Schatzkiste*

As Stanley stared at the glittering night sky, he thought there was no place he would rather be. He was glad Zero put the shoes on the parked car. He was glad they fell from the overpass and hit him on the head.

When the shoes first fell from the sky, he remembered thinking that destiny had struck him. Now, he thought so again. It was more than a coincidence. It had to be destiny.

Maybe they wouldn't have to return to Camp Green Lake, he thought. Maybe they could make it past the camp, then follow the dirt road back to civilization. They could fill the sack with onions, and the three jars with water. And he had his canteen as well.

They could refill their jars and canteen at the camp. Maybe sneak into the kitchen and get some food.

He doubted any counselors were still on guard. Everyone had to think they were dead. Buzzard food.

It would mean living the rest of his life as a fugitive. The police would always be after him. At least he could call his parents and tell them he was still alive. But he couldn't go visit them, in case the police were watching the apartment. Although, if everyone thought he was dead, they wouldn't bother to watch the apartment. He would have to somehow get a new identity.

Now, I'm really thinking crazy, he thought. He wondered if a crazy person wonders if he's crazy.

But even as he thought this, an even crazier idea kept popping into his head. He knew it was too crazy to even consider. Still, if he was going to be a fugitive for the rest of his life, it would help to have some money, perhaps a treasure chest full of money.

You're crazy! he told himself. Besides, just because he found a lipstick container with *KB* on it, that didn't mean there was treasure buried there.

It was crazy. It was all part of his crazy feeling of happiness. Or maybe it was destiny.

He reached over and shook Zero's arm. "Hey, Zero," he whispered.

"Huh?" Zero muttered.

"Zero, wake up."

"What?" Zero raised up his head. "What is it?"

"You want to dig one more hole?" Stanley asked him.

43

"We weren't always homeless," Zero said. "I remember a yellow room."

"How old were you when you ..." Stanley started to ask, but couldn't find the right words. "... moved out?"

"I don't know. I must have been real little, because I don't remember too much. I don't remember moving out. I remember standing in a crib, with my mother singing to me. She held my wrists and made my hands clap together. She used to sing that song to me. That one you sang ... It was different, though ..."

crib a bed with high sides for a baby or young child

Zero spoke slowly, as if searching his brain for memories and clues. "And then later I know we lived on the street, but I don't know why we left the house. I'm pretty sure it was a house, and not an apartment. I know my room was yellow."

It was late afternoon. They were resting in the shadow of the Thumb. They had spent the morning picking onions and putting them in the sack. It didn't take long, but long enough so that they had to wait another day before heading down the mountain.

They wanted to leave at the first hint of daylight, so they'd have plenty of time to make it to Camp Green Lake before dark. Stanley wanted to be sure he could find the right hole. Then, they would hide by it until everyone went to sleep.

They would dig for as long as it seemed safe, and not a second longer. And then, treasure or no treasure, they'd head up the dirt road. If it was absolutely safe, they'd try to steal some food and water from the camp kitchen.

"I'm good at sneaking in and out of places," Zero had said.

"Remember," Stanley had warned. "The door to the Wreck Room squeaks."

to squeak here: *quietschen*

Now he lay on his back, trying to save his strength for the long days ahead. He wondered what happened to Zero's parents, but he didn't ask. Zero didn't like answering questions. It was better to just let him talk when he felt like it.

Stanley thought about his own parents. In her last letter, his mom was worried that they might be evicted from their apartment because of the smell of burning sneakers. They could easily become homeless as well.

to evict to expel sb from property by a process of law
eviction the expulsion of sb from property by a process of law
evictee sb who is expelled from property by a process of law

Again, he wondered if they'd been told that he ran away from camp. Were they told that he was dead?

image here: a picture in your mind

inexplicable unable to be explained

An image appeared in his head of his parents hugging each other and crying. He tried not to think about it.

Instead he tried to recapture the feelings he'd had the night before – the inexplicable feeling of happiness, the sense of destiny. But those feelings didn't return.

He just felt scared.

***

to dunk to dip in liquid

to cram *vollstopfen*

The next morning they headed down the mountain. They'd dunked their caps in the water hole before putting them on their heads. Zero held the shovel, and Stanley carried the sack, which was crammed with onions and the three jars of water. They left the pieces of the broken jar on the mountain.

"This is where I found the shovel," Stanley said, pointing out a patch of weeds.

Zero turned and looked up toward the top of the mountain. "That's a long way."

"You were light," Stanley said. "You'd already thrown up everything that was inside your stomach."

to slip to unexpectedly lose your balance or foothold
to slide down to move downwards after losing your balance or foothold

vine *Kletterpflanze*

He shifted the sack from one shoulder to the other. It was heavy. He stepped on a loose rock, slipped, then fell hard. The next thing he knew he was sliding down the steep side of the mountain. He dropped the sack, and onions spilled around him.

He slid into a patch of weeds and grabbed onto a thorny vine. The vine ripped out of the earth, but slowed him enough so that he was able to stop himself.

"Are you all right?" Zero asked from above.

Stanley groaned as he pulled a thorn out of the palm of his hand. "Yeah," he said. He was all right. He was worried more about the jars of water.

to retrieve to get or fetch back

pant leg the part of a pair of trousers that covers a person's leg

Styrofoam *Styropor*

★ **to recover** here: to get back; find again

Zero climbed down after him, retrieving the sack along the way. Stanley pulled some thorns out of his pant legs.

The jars hadn't broken. The onions had protected them, like Styrofoam packing material. "Glad you didn't do that when you were carrying me," Zero said.

They'd lost about a third of the onions, but recovered many of them as they continued down the mountain. When they reached the bottom, the sun was just rising above the lake. They walked directly toward it.

Soon they stood on the edge of a cliff, looking down on the dry lake bed. Stanley wasn't sure, but he thought he could see the remains of the *Mary Lou* off in the distance.

"You thirsty?" Stanley asked.

"No," said Zero. "How about you."

"No," Stanley lied. He didn't want to be the first one to take a drink. Although they didn't mention it, it had become a kind of challenge between him and Zero.

They climbed down into the frying pan. It was a different spot from where they had climbed up. They eased themselves down from one ledge to another, and let themselves slide in other places, being especially careful with the sack.

Stanley could no longer see the *Mary Lou*, but headed in what he thought was the right direction. As the sun rose, so did the familiar haze of heat and dirt.

"You thirsty?" Zero asked.

"No," said Stanley.

"Because you have three full jars of water," said Zero. "I thought maybe it was getting too heavy for you. If you drink some, it will lighten your load."

"I'm not thirsty," said Stanley. "But if you want a drink, I'll give you some."

"I'm not thirsty," said Zero. "I was just worried about you."

Stanley smiled. "I'm a camel," he said.

They walked for what seemed like a very long time, and still never came across the *Mary Lou*. Stanley was pretty sure they were heading in the right direction. He remembered that when they left the boat, they were headed toward the setting sun. Now they were headed toward the rising sun. He knew the sun didn't rise and set exactly in the east and west; more southeast and southwest, but he wasn't sure how that made a difference.

His throat felt as if it was coated with sandpaper. "You sure you're not thirsty?" he asked.

"Not me," said Zero. His voice was dry and raspy.

When they did finally take a drink, they agreed to do it at the same time. Zero, who was now carrying the sack, set it down and took out two jars, giving one to Stanley. They decided to save the canteen for last, since it couldn't accidentally break.

"You know I'm not thirsty," Stanley said, as he unscrewed the lid. "I'm just drinking so you will."

"I'm just drinking so you will," said Zero.

They clinked the jars together and, each watching the other, poured the water into their stubborn mouths.

Zero was the first to spot the *Mary Lou*, maybe a quarter mile away, and just a little off to the right. They headed for it.

It wasn't even noon yet when they reached the boat. They sat against the shady side and rested.

haze *Dunst*

to coat to cover with a layer of sth

raspy harsh and rough

to clink to make a light, sharp ringing sound

***stubborn** obstinate; *stur, starrköpfig*
stubborn as a mule very stubborn
stubbornness obstinacy

shady sheltered from the sun

What does Zero tell Stanley about his mother?

"I don't know what happened to my mother," Zero said. "She left and never came back."

Stanley peeled an onion.

"She couldn't always take me with her," Zero said. "Sometimes she had to do things by herself."

Stanley had the feeling that Zero was explaining things to himself.

"She'd tell me to wait in a certain place for her. When I was real little, I had to wait in small areas, like on a porch step or a doorway. 'Now don't leave here until I get back,' she'd say.

"I never liked it when she left. I had a stuffed animal, a little giraffe, and I'd hug it the whole time she was gone. When I got bigger I was allowed to stay in bigger areas. Like, 'Stay on this block.' Or, 'Don't leave the park.' But even then, I still held Jaffy."

Stanley guessed that Jaffy was the name of Zero's giraffe.

"And then one day she didn't come back," Zero said. His voice sounded suddenly hollow. "I waited for her at Laney Park."

"Laney Park," said Stanley. "I've been there."

"You know the playscape?" asked Zero.

"Yeah. I've played on it."

"I waited there for more than a month," said Zero. "You know that tunnel that you crawl through, between the slide and the swinging bridge? That's where I slept."

They ate four onions apiece and drank about half a jar of water. Stanley stood up and looked around. Everything looked the same in all directions.

"When I left camp, I was heading straight toward Big Thumb," he said. "I saw the boat off to the right. So that means we have to turn a little to the left."

Zero was lost in thought. "What? Okay," he said.

They headed out. It was Stanley's turn to carry the sack.

"Some kids had a birthday party," Zero said. "I guess it was about two weeks after my mother left. There was a picnic table next to the playscape and balloons were tied to it. The kids looked to be the same age as me. One girl said hi to me and asked me if I wanted to play. I wanted to, but I didn't. I knew I didn't belong at the party, even though it wasn't their playscape. There was this one mother who kept staring at me like I was some kind of monster. Then later a boy asked me if I wanted a piece of cake, but then that same mother told me, 'Go away!' and she told all the kids to stay away from me, so I never got the piece of cake. I ran away so fast, I forgot Jaffy."

"Did you ever find him – it?"

porch veranda

hollow here: weaker and less deep

playscape an area designed for play and enjoyment in a public park

slide *Rutsche*

★ **to stare at** to look at for a long time

For a moment, Zero didn't answer. Then he said, "He wasn't real."

Stanley thought again about his own parents, how awful it would be for them to never know if he was dead or alive. He realized that was how Zero must have felt, not knowing what happened to his own mother. He wondered why Zero never mentioned his father.

"Hold on," Zero said, stopping abruptly. "We're going the wrong way."

"No, this is right," said Stanley.

"You were heading toward Big Thumb when you saw the boat off to your right," said Zero. "That means we should have turned right when we left the boat."

"You sure?"

Zero drew a diagram in the dirt.

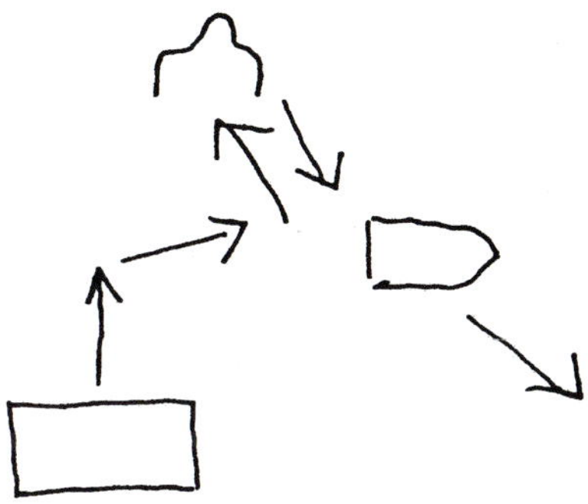

Stanley still wasn't sure.

"We need to go this way," Zero said, first drawing a line on the map and then heading that way himself.

Stanley followed. It didn't feel right to him, but Zero seemed sure.

Sometime in the middle of the afternoon, a cloud drifted across the sky and blocked out the sun. It was a welcome relief. Once again, Stanley felt that destiny was on his side.

Zero stopped and held out his arm to stop Stanley, too.

"Listen," Zero whispered.

Stanley didn't hear anything.

They continued walking very quietly and Stanley began to make out the faint sounds of Camp Green Lake. They were still too far away to see the camp, but he could hear a blend of indistinct voices. As they got closer he occasionally could hear Mr. Sir's distinctive bark.

They walked slowly and quietly, aware that sounds travel in both directions.

★**abrupt** sudden, unexpected
abruptness a rude and insulting manner

★ **relief** the feeling of happiness that you have when sth unpleasant stops or does not happen

faint soft and unclear

blend a mixture

distinctive characteristic; identifiable

cluster a grouping of sth

They approached a cluster of holes. "Let's wait here, until they go in," said Zero.

Stanley nodded. He checked to make sure there was nothing living in it, then climbed down into a hole. Zero climbed into the one next to him.

Despite having gone the wrong way for a while, it hadn't taken them nearly as long as Stanley had expected. Now, they just had to wait.

The sun cut through the cloud, and Stanley felt its rays beating down on him. But soon more clouds filled the sky, shading Stanley and his hole.

He waited until he was certain the last of the campers had finished for the day.

Then he waited a little longer.

compound an area that contains a group of buildings

dizzy *schwindelig*

to summon to gather together; to call up

As quietly as possible, he and Zero climbed up out of their holes and crept toward camp. Stanley held the sack in front of him, cradled in his arms, instead of over his shoulder, to keep the jars from clanking against each other. A wave of terror rushed over him when he saw the compound – the tents, the Wreck Room, the Warden's cabin under the two oak trees. The fear made him dizzy. He took a breath, summoned his courage, and continued.

"That's the one," he whispered, pointing out the hole where he had found the gold tube. It was still about fifty yards away, but Stanley was pretty sure it was the right hole. There was no need to risk going any closer.

adjacent next to or near

They climbed down into adjacent holes, and waited for the camp to fall asleep.

44

to creak to make a harsh squeaking sound

Stanley tried to sleep, not knowing when he'd get the chance again. He heard the showers and, later, the sounds of dinner. He heard the creaking of the Wreck Room door. His fingers drummed against the side of the hole. He heard his own heart beat.

He took a drink from the canteen. He had given Zero the water jars. They each had a good supply of onions.

He wasn't sure how long he remained in the hole, maybe five hours. He was surprised when he heard Zero whispering for him to wake up. He didn't think he'd fallen asleep. If he had, he thought it must have just been for the last five minutes. Although, when he opened his eyes, he was surprised how dark it was.

There was only one light on at camp, in the office. The sky was cloudy, so there was very little starlight. Stanley could see a sliver of a moon, which appeared and disappeared among the clouds.

He carefully led Zero to the hole, which was hard to find in the darkness. He stumbled over a small pile of dirt. "I think this is it," he whispered.

"You *think*?" Zero asked.

"It's it," said Stanley, sounding more certain than he really was. He climbed down. Zero handed him the shovel.

Stanley stuck the shovel into the dirt at the bottom of the hole and stepped on the back of the blade. He felt it sink beneath his weight. He scooped out some dirt and tossed it off to the side. Then he brought the shovel back down.

Zero watched for a while. "I'm going to try to refill the water jars," he said.

Stanley took a deep breath and exhaled. "Be careful," he said, then continued digging.

It was so dark, he couldn't even see the end of his shovel. For all he knew he could be digging up gold and diamonds instead of dirt. He brought each shovelful close to his face, to try to see if anything was there, before dumping it out of the hole.

As he made the hole deeper, it became harder to lift the dirt up and out. It was five feet deep before he even started. He decided to use his efforts to make it wider instead.

This made more sense, he told himself. If Kate Barlow had buried a treasure chest, she probably wouldn't have been able to dig much deeper, so why should he?

Of course, Kate Barlow probably had a whole gang of thieves helping her.

"You want some breakfast?"

Stanley jumped at the sound of Zero's voice. He hadn't heard him approach.

Zero handed down a box of cereal. Stanley carefully poured some cereal into his mouth. He didn't want to put his dirty hands inside the box. He nearly gagged on the ultra-sweet taste. They were sugar-frosted flakes, and after eating nothing but onions for more than a week, he had trouble adjusting to the flavor. He washed them down with a swig of water.

Zero took over the digging. Stanley sifted his fingers through the fresh piles of dirt, in case he had missed anything. He

sliver a small narrow portion

★**to exhale** to breathe out
exhalation the act of breathing out air

to bury to place in the earth and cover with soil

cereal food made from grain and often eaten for breakfast
to gag to almost throw up because you find sth disgusting

to adjust here: to get used to sth new
a swig a large swallow

flashlight torch
pebble a small, smooth rounded stone
spigot a tap, esp. on the outside of a building
to cave in to collapse in on itself
to bounce off here: *abprallen*
to chip to break off in small pieces
to flake away to fall off in small flakes
pronounced easily seen
a foot and a half about 45 cm

What does Stanley find in the hole he is digging?

texture the appearance and feel of a surface

★astonishment extreme surprise, amazement
to astonish to surprise, amaze
astonishing surprising, amazing

to collapse to fall down or cave in suddenly
to scrape to remove by rubbing a sharp tool against a hard surface
to not budge to not move even a tiny bit

wished he had a flashlight. A diamond no bigger than a pebble would be worth thousands of dollars. Yet there was no way he'd see it.

They finished the water that Zero had gotten from the spigot by the showers. Stanley said he'd go fill the jars again, but Zero insisted that he do it instead. "No offense, but you make too much noise when you walk. You're too big."

Stanley returned to the hole. As the hole grew wider, parts of the surface kept caving in. They were running out of room. To make it much wider, they would first have to move some of the surrounding dirt piles out of the way. He wondered how much time they had before the camp woke up.

"How's it going?" Zero asked when he returned with the water.

Stanley shrugged one shoulder. He brought the shovel down the side of the hole, shaving off a slice of the dirt wall. As he did so, he felt the shovel bounce off something hard.

"What was that?" Zero asked.

Stanley didn't know. He moved his shovel up and down the side of the hole. As the dirt chipped and flaked away, the hard object became more pronounced.

It was sticking out of the side of the hole, about a foot and a half from the bottom. He felt it with his hands.

"What is it?" Zero asked.

He could just feel a corner of it. Most of it was still buried. It had the cool, smooth texture of metal. "I think I might have found the treasure chest," he said. His voice was filled more with astonishment than with excitement.

"Really?" asked Zero.

"I think so," Stanley said.

The hole was wide enough for him to hold the shovel lengthwise and dig sideways into the wall. He knew he had to dig very carefully. He didn't want the side of the hole to collapse, along with the huge pile of dirt directly above it.

He scraped at the dirt wall, until he exposed one entire side of the box-like object. He ran his fingers over it. It felt to be about eight inches tall, and almost two feet wide. He had no way of knowing how far into the earth it extended. He tried pulling it out, but it wouldn't budge.

He was afraid that the only way to get to it was to start back up at the surface, and dig down. They didn't have time for that.

"I'm going to try to dig a hole underneath it," he said. "Then maybe I can pull it down and slip it out."

"Go for it," said Zero.

Stanley jammed the shovel into the bottom edge of his hole, and carefully began to dig a tunnel underneath the metal object. He hoped it didn't cave in.

Occasionally he'd stop, stoop down, and try to feel the far end of the box. But even when the tunnel was as long as his arm, he still couldn't feel the other side.

Once again he tried pulling it out, but it was firmly in the ground. If he pulled too hard, he feared, he'd cause a cave-in. He knew that when he was ready to pull it out, he would have to do it quickly, before the ground above it collapsed.

As his tunnel grew deeper and wider – and more precarious – Stanley was able to feel latches on one end of the box, and then a leather handle. It wasn't really a box. "I think it might be some kind of metal suitcase," he told Zero.

"Can you pry it loose with the shovel?" Zero suggested.

"I'm afraid the side of the hole will collapse."

"You might as well give it a try," said Zero.

Stanley took a sip of water. "Might as well," he said.

He forced the tip of the shovel between the dirt and the top of the metal case and tried to wedge it free. He wished he could see what he was doing.

He worked the end of the shovel, back and forth, up and down, until he felt the suitcase fall free. Then he felt the dirt come piling down on top of it.

But it wasn't a huge cave-in. As he knelt down in the hole, he could tell that only a small portion of the earth had collapsed.

He dug with his hands until he found the leather handle, and then he pulled the suitcase up and out of the dirt. "I got it!" he exclaimed.

It was heavy. He handed it up to Zero.

"You did it," Zero said, taking it from him.

"We did it," said Stanley.

He gathered his remaining strength, and tried to pull himself up out of the hole. Suddenly, a bright light was shining in his face.

"Thank you," said the Warden. "You boys have been a big help."

to jam here: to push sth tightly into a small space

precarious liable to failure or catastrophe; insecure
precariousness extreme danger and insecurity

latch here: a lock on a suitcase, box or trunk

to pry loose to use a lever of some kind to force sth out from its surroundings

to wedge free to force apart as if with a wedge (*Keil*)

45

The beam of the flashlight was directed away from Stanley's eyes and onto Zero, who was sitting on his knees. The suitcase was on his lap.

Mr. Pendanski was holding the flashlight. Mr. Sir stood next to him with his gun drawn and pointed in the same direction. Mr. Sir was barefoot and bare-chested, wearing only his pajama bottoms.

The Warden moved toward Zero. She was also in her bed clothes, wearing an extra-long T-shirt. Unlike Mr. Sir, however, she had on her boots.

Mr. Pendanski was the only one fully dressed. Perhaps he had been on guard duty.

to be on guard duty *Wachdienst haben*

Off in the distance, Stanley could see two more flashlights bobbing toward them in the darkness. He felt helpless in the hole.

to bob to move up and down repeatedly

Explain the terrified reaction of the people when they see the lizards.

"You boys arrived just in the nick –" the Warden started to say. She stopped talking and she stopped walking. Then she slowly backed away.

in the nick (of time) at the last possible moment

A lizard had crawled up on top of the suitcase. Its big red eyes glowed in the beam of the flashlight. Its mouth was open, and Stanley could see its white tongue moving in and out between its black teeth.

lizard *Eidechse*

Zero sat as still as a statue.

A second lizard crawled up over the side of the suitcase and stopped less than an inch away from Zero's little finger.

Stanley was afraid to look, and afraid not to. He wondered if he should try to scramble out of the hole before the lizards turned on him, but he didn't want to cause any commotion.

to scramble out to move or climb out quickly, esp. on your hands and knees
commotion a noisy disturbance that attracts attention

The second lizard crawled across Zero's fingers and halfway up his arm.

It occurred to Stanley that the lizards were probably on the suitcase when he handed it to Zero.

"There's another one!" gasped Mr. Pendanski. He shined the flashlight on the box of Frosted Flakes, which lay on its side beside Stanley's hole. A lizard was crawling out of it.

The light also illuminated Stanley's hole. He glanced downward and had to force himself to suppress a scream. He was standing in a lizard nest. He felt the scream explode inside him.

***to suppress** to hold in check; to restrain
suppression the act or process of holding back sth or sb
suppressive restrictive

He could see six lizards. There were three on the ground, two on his left legs and one on his right sneaker.

He tried to remain very still. Something was crawling up the back of his neck.

Three other counselors approached the area. Stanley heard one say, "What's going –" and then whisper, "Oh my God."

"What do we do?" asked Mr. Pendanski.

"We wait," said the Warden. "It won't be very long."

"At least we'll have a body to give that woman," said Mr. Pendanski.

"She's going to ask a lot of questions," said Mr. Sir. "And this time she'll have the A.G. with her."

"Let her ask her questions," said the Warden. "Just so long as I have the suitcase, I don't care what happens. Do you know how long ..." Her voice trailed off, then started up again. "When I was little I'd watch my parents dig holes, every weekend and holiday. When I got bigger, I had to dig, too. Even on Christmas."

to trail off to become gradually quieter and then stop altogether

Stanley felt tiny claws into the side of his face as the lizard pulled itself off his neck and up past his chin.

claw *Kralle*

"It won't be long now," the Warden said.

Stanley could hear his heart beat. Each beat told him he was still alive, at least for one more second.

46

Five hundred seconds later, his heart was still beating.

Mr. Pendanski screamed. The lizard which had been in the cereal box was springing toward him.

Mr. Sir shot it in midair.

Stanley felt the blast shatter the air around him. The lizards scurried frantically across his very still body. He did not flinch. A lizard ran across his closed mouth.

He glanced at Zero and Zero's eyes met his. Somehow they were both still alive, at least for one more second, one more heartbeat.

blast here: explosive discharge produced by the bullet
to shatter here: to burst
to scurry to move quickly with light, running steps
to flinch to draw back suddenly, esp. due to pain, shock, etc.

Mr. Sir lit a cigarette.

"I thought you quit," said one of the other counselors.

"Yeah, well, sometimes sunflower seeds just won't cut it." He took a long drag on his cigarette. "I'm going to have nightmares the rest of my life."

"Maybe we should just shoot them," suggested Mr. Pendanski.

drag a puff on a cigarette, pipe or cigar
★ **nightmare** a terrifying dream

grim cruel, macabre

grave the place in the ground where a dead body is buried

to initiate to begin or be the cause of sth

to release to free a person from captivity or imprisonment

to etch to imprint very clearly

to bundle up to dress warmly and snugly

mitten *Fausthandschuh*

fleck a small spot

cheery happy, cheerful

lawyer sb whose job is to advise people about laws, write formal agreements, or represent people in court

"Who?" asked a counselor. "The lizards or the kids?"

Mr. Pendanski laughed grimly. "The kids are going to die anyway." He laughed again. "At least we got plenty of graves to choose from."

"We've got time," said the Warden. "I've waited this long, I can wait another few ..." Her voice trailed off.

Stanley felt a lizard crawl in and out of his pocket.

"We're going to keep our story simple," said the Warden. "That woman's going to ask a lot of questions. The A.G. will most likely initiate an investigation. So this is what happened: Stanley tried to run away in the night, fell in a hole, and the lizards got him. That's it. We're not even going to give them Zero's body. As far as anybody knows, Zero doesn't exist. Like Mom said, we got plenty of graves to choose from."

"Why would he run away if he knew he was getting released today?" asked Mr. Pendanski.

"Who knows? He's crazy. That was why we couldn't release him yesterday. He was delirious, and we had to keep watch over him so he wouldn't hurt himself or anybody else."

"She's not going to like it," said Mr. Pendanski.

"She's not going to like anything we tell her," said the Warden. She stared at Zero and at the suitcase. "Why aren't you dead yet?" she asked.

Stanley only half listened to the talk of the counselors. He didn't know who "that woman" was or what "A.G." meant. He didn't even realize they were initials. It sounded like one word, "Age-ee." His mind was focused on the tiny claws that moved up and down his skin and through his hair.

He tried to think about other things. He didn't want to die with the images of the Warden, Mr. Sir, and the lizards etched into his brain. Instead, he tried to see his mother's face.

His brain took him back to a time when he was very little, all bundled up in a snowsuit. He and his mother were walking, hand in hand, mitten in mitten, when they both slipped on some ice and fell and rolled down a snow-covered hillside. They ended up at the bottom of the hill. He remembered he almost cried, but instead he laughed. His mother laughed, too. He could feel the same light-headed feeling he felt then, dizzy from rolling down the hill. He felt the sharp coldness of the snow against his ear. He could see flecks of snow on his mother's bright and cheery face.

This was where he wanted to be when he died.

"Hey, Caveman, guess what?" said Mr. Sir. "You're innocent, after all. I thought you'd like to know that. Your lawyer came to get you yesterday. Too bad you weren't here."

The words meant nothing to Stanley, who was still in the snow. He and his mother climbed back up the hill and rolled down again, this time on purpose. Later they had hot chocolate with lots of melted marshmallows.

"It's getting close to 4:30," said Mr. Pendanski. "They'll be waking up."

The Warden told the counselors to return to the tents. She told them to give the campers breakfast and to make sure they didn't talk to anyone. As long as they did as they were told, they wouldn't have to dig any more holes. If they talked, they would be severely punished.

"How should we say they will be punished?" one of the counselors asked.

"Let them use their imaginations," said the Warden.

Stanley watched the counselors return to the tents, leaving only the Warden and Mr. Sir behind. He knew the Warden didn't care whether the campers dug any more holes or not. She'd found what she was looking for.

He glanced at Zero. A lizard was perched on his shoulder.

Zero remained perfectly still except for his right hand, which slowly formed into a fist. Then he raised his thumb, giving Stanley the thumbs-up sign.

Stanley thought back to what Mr. Sir had said to him earlier, and the bits of conversation he'd overheard. He tried to make sense out of it. Mr. Sir had said something about a lawyer, but Stanley knew his parents couldn't afford a lawyer.

His legs were sore from remaining rigid for so long. Standing still was more strenuous than walking. He slowly allowed himself to lean against the side of the hole.

The lizards didn't seem to mind.

➊ Describe the images that cross Stanley's mind in that moment of extreme danger.

severe harsh, unnecessarily extreme

★ **imagination** the ability to form mental images und think of creative ideas

to perch to sit up high as if resting on a branch

★**rigid** not able to be bent, inflexible, stiff
rigidity the property of a substance that renders it inflexible, stiff, or non-pliable

sore hurting, in pain

strenuous requiring a great deal of effort or energy

47

The sun was up, and Stanley's heart was still beating. There were eight lizards in the hole with him. Each one had exactly eleven yellow spots.

The Warden had dark circles under her eyes from lack of sleep, and lines across her forehead and face which seemed exaggerated in the stark morning light.

Her skin looked blotchy.

★**to exaggerate** to make sth appear to be greater or more impressive than it really is
exaggeration the act of overstating

blotchy marked with irregularly-shaped spots and red patches

"Satan," said Zero.

Stanley looked at him, unsure if Zero had even spoken or if he'd just imagined it.

"Why don't you go see if you can take the suitcase from Zero," the Warden suggested.

"Yeah, right," said Mr. Sir.

"The lizards obviously aren't hungry." said the Warden.

"Then you go get the suitcase," said Mr. Sir.

They waited.

"Sa-tan lee," said Zero.

tarantula a large, hairy spider that has a painful bite

Sometime later Stanley saw a tarantula crawl across the dirt, not too far from his hole. He had never seen a tarantula before, but there was no doubt what it was. He was momentarily fascinated by it, as its big hairy body moved slowly and steadily along.

"Look, a tarantula," said Mr. Sir, also fascinated.

"I've never seen one," said the Warden. "Except in –"

sting *Stich*

Stanley suddenly felt a sharp sting the side of his neck.

The lizard hadn't bitten him, however. It was merely pushing off.

to pounce to jump on suddenly, esp. to attack prey

It leapt off Stanley's neck and pounced on the tarantula. The last Stanley saw of it was one hairy leg sticking out of the lizard's mouth.

"Not hungry, huh?" said Mr. Sir.

Stanley tried to return to the snow, but it was harder to get there when the sun was up.

As the sun rose, the lizards moved lower in the hole, keeping mainly in the shade. They were no longer on his head and shoulders but had moved down to his stomach, legs, and feet.

He couldn't see any lizards on Zero, but believed there were two, between Zero's knees, shaded from the sun by the suitcase.

"How are you doing?" Stanley asked quietly. He didn't whisper, but his voice was dry and raspy.

numb without feeling; *taub*

"My legs are numb," said Zero.

"I'm going to try to climb out of the hole," Stanley said.

ankle the joint connecting the foot and leg

As he tried to pull himself up, using just his arms, he felt a claw into his ankle. He gently eased himself back down.

"Is your last name your first name backward?" Zero asked.

Stanley stared at him in amazement. Had he been working on that all night?

He heard the sound of approaching cars.

Mr. Sir and the Warden heard it as well.
"You think it's them?" asked the Warden.
"It ain't Girl Scouts selling cookies," said Mr. Sir.

He heard the cars come to a stop, and the doors open and shut. A little while later he saw Mr. Pendanski and two strangers coming across the lake. One was a tall man in a business suit and cowboy hat. The other was a short woman holding a briefcase. The woman had to take three steps for every two taken by the man.
"Stanley Yelnats?" she called, moving out ahead of the others.
"I suggest you don't come any closer," said Mr. Sir.
"You can't stop me," she snapped, then took a second glance at him, wearing pajama pants and nothing else. "We'll get you out of there, Stanley," she said. "Don't you worry." She appeared to be Hispanic, with straight black hair and dark eyes. She spoke with a little bit of a Mexican accent, trilling her r's.
"What in tarnation?" the tall man exclaimed, as he came up behind her.
She turned on him. "I'm telling you right now, if any harm comes to him, we will be filing charges not only against Ms. Walker and Camp Green Lake but the entire state of Texas as well. Child abuse. False imprisonment. Torture."
The man was more than a head taller than she, and was able to look directly over her as he spoke to the Warden.
"How long have they been in there?"
"All night, as you can see by the way we're dressed. They snuck into my cabin while I was asleep, and stole my suitcase. I chased after them, and they ran out here and fell into the lizards' nest. I don't know what they were thinking."
"That's not true!" Stanley said.
"Stanley, as your attorney, I advise you not to say anything," said the woman, "until you and I have had a chance to talk in private."
Stanley wondered why the Warden lied about the suitcase. He wondered who it legally belonged to. That was one thing he wanted to ask his lawyer, if she really was his lawyer.
"It's a miracle they're still alive," said the tall man.
"Yes, it is," the Warden agreed, with just a trace of disappointment in her voice.
"And they better come out of this alive," Stanley's lawyer warned. "This wouldn't have happened if you'd released him to me yesterday."
"It wouldn't have happened if he wasn't a thief," said the Warden. "I told him he would be set free today, and I guess

briefcase a light, leather case for carrying documents

to snap to answer abruptly in an angry way

in tarnation hell (used as a euphemism)
★ **harm** damage; injury
to file charges *Strafanzeige erstatten*
child abuse *Kindesmissbrauch*

★**imprisonment** the state of being put in prison
to imprison to put in prison
to imprison sb in sth to lock sb up in sth

★ **torture** the act of treating sb cruelly as a punishment

to sneak, snuck, snuck to go quietly and secretly

★ **attorney** lawyer

★ **legal** in accordance with the law

trace here: a tiny amount that is barely noticeable

valuables *Wertsachen*

authorization here: official permission to do sth

court order a legal document issued by a judge telling sb what they must do or alternatively what they are not allowed to do.

to authenticate *beglaubigen*

judge public official with the authority to hear cases in a court of law and pronounce judgement upon them

to sentence to pronounce a judgement on a convicted person in a court of law
sentence court judgement
to pass sentence on someone to read out the punishment for a convicted criminal

★ **legitimate** in accordance with the law
custody care, supervision
hospitalized receiving medical care in a hospital
delirium mental confusion due to illness, shock, high fever, etc.
★ **to rant** to talk wildly in a loud and uncontrolled manner
to rave to talk in an angry and incoherent manner

to steady oneself to regain one's balance
steadiness freedom from wavering or indecision
steady firmly in position or place

to jerk free to pull away abruptly
red-handed in the act of committing a crime

he decided he'd try to take some of my valuables with him. He's been delirious for the last week."

"Why didn't you release him when she came to you yesterday?" the tall man asked.

"She didn't have proper authorization", said the Warden.

"I had a court order!"

"It was not authenticated," the Warden said.

"Authenticated? It was signed by the judge who sentenced him."

"I needed authentication from the Attorney General," said the Warden. "How do I know it's legitimate? The boys in my custody have proven themselves dangerous to society. Am I supposed to just turn them loose any time someone hands me a piece of paper?"

"Yes," said the woman. "If it's a court order."

"Stanley has been hospitalized for the last few days," the Warden explained. "He's been suffering from hallucinations and delirium. Ranting and raving. He was in no condition to leave. The fact that he was trying to steal from me on the day before his release proves ..."

Stanley tried to climb out of his hole, using mostly his arms so as not to disturb the lizards too much. As he pulled himself upward, the lizards moved downward, keeping out of the sun's direct rays. He swung his legs up and over, and the last of the lizards hopped off.

"Thank God!" exclaimed the Warden. She started toward him, then stopped.

A lizard crawled out of his pocket and down his leg.

Stanley was overcome by a rush of dizziness and almost fell over. He steadied himself, then reached down, took hold of Zero's arm, and helped him slowly to his feet. Zero still held the suitcase.

The lizards, which had been hiding under it, scurried quickly into the hole.

Stanley and Zero staggered away.

The Warden rushed to them. She hugged Zero.

"Thank God, you're alive," she said, as she tried to take the suitcase from him.

He jerked it free. "It belongs to Stanley," he said.

"Don't cause any more trouble," the Warden warned. "You stole it from my cabin, and you've been caught red-handed. If I press charges, Stanley might have to return to prison. Now I'm willing in view of all the circumstances, to –"

"It's got his name on it," said Zero.

Stanley's lawyer pushed past the tall man to have a look.
"See," Zero showed her. "Stanley Yelnats."
Stanley looked, too. There, in big black letters, was STANLEY YELNATS.
The tall man looked over the heads of the others at the name on the suitcase. "You say he stole it from your cabin?"
The Warden stared at it in disbelief. "That's im ... imposs ... It's imposs ..." She couldn't even say it.

48

They slowly walked back to camp. The tall man was the Texas Attorney General, the chief law enforcement officer for the state. Stanley's lawyer was named Ms. Morengo.
Stanley held the suitcase. He was so tired he couldn't think straight. He felt as if he was walking in a dream, not quite able to comprehend what was going on around him.
They stopped in front of the camp office. Mr. Sir went inside to get Stanley's belongings. The Attorney General told Mr. Pendanski to get the boys something to drink and eat.
The Warden seemed as dazed as Stanley. "You can't even read," she said to Zero.
Zero said nothing.
Ms. Morengo put a hand on Stanley's shoulder and told him to hang in there. He would be seeing his parents soon.
She was shorter than Stanley, but somehow gave the appearance of being tall.
Mr. Pendanski returned with two cartons of orange juice and two bagels. Stanley drank the juice but didn't feel like eating anything.
"Wait!" the Warden exclaimed. "I didn't say they stole the suitcase. It's *his* suitcase, obviously, but he put my things from my cabin inside it."
"That isn't what you said earlier," said Ms. Morengo.
"What's in the suitcase?" the Warden asked Stanley. "Tell us what's in it, then we'll open it and see!"
Stanley didn't know what to do.
"Stanley, as your lawyer, I advise you not to open your suitcase," said Ms. Morengo.
"He has to open it!" said the Warden. "I have the right to check the personal property of any of the detainees. How do

chief law enforcement officer Attorney General of a state; *oberster Staatsanwalt*

★ **to comprehend** to understand

dazed confused; unable to think properly

★**appearance** the outward or visible aspect of a person or thing
to appear to seem

bagel *weiches, ringförmiges Brötchen*

detainee prisoner

witness sb who sees an event happening, esp. a crime or accident
jurisdiction area of authority and control

I know there aren't drugs or weapons in there? He stole a car, too! I've got witnesses!" She was nearly hysterical.

"He is no longer under your jurisdiction," said Stanley's lawyer.

"He has not been officially released," said the Warden. "Open the suitcase, Stanley!"

"Do not open it," said Stanley's lawyer.

Stanley did nothing.

Mr. Sir returned from the office with Stanley's backpack and clothes.

The Attorney General handed Ms. Morengo a sheet of paper. "You're free to go," he said to Stanley. "I know you're anxious to get out of here, so you can just keep the orange suit as a souvenir. Or burn it, whatever you want. Good luck, Stanley."

***anxious** wanting very much for sth to happen quickly

He reached out his hand to shake, but Ms. Morengo hurried Stanley away. "C'mon, Stanley," she said. "We have a lot to talk about."

Stanley stopped and turned to look at Zero. He couldn't just leave him here.

Zero gave him thumbs-up.

"I can't leave Hector," Stanley said.

"I suggest we go," said his lawyer with a sense of urgency in her voice.

***urgency** the need for speedy action or attention
urgent very important and needing to be dealt with immediately
to urge 1. to push or force along; 2. to strongly suggest that sb does sth

"I'll be okay," said Zero. His eyes shifted toward Mr. Pendanski on one side of him, then to the Warden and Mr. Sir on the other.

"There's nothing I can do for your friend," said Ms. Morengo. "You are released pursuant to an order from the judge."

pursuant to in accordance with

"They'll kill him," said Stanley.

"Your friend is not in danger," said the Attorney General. "There's going to be an investigation into everything that's happened here. For the present, I am taking charge of the camp."

investigation analysis; enquiry
to take charge to be or become responsible for

"C'mon, Stanley," said his lawyer. "Your parents are waiting."

Stanley stayed where he was.

Why is Stanley reluctant to leave after his release? ➔

His lawyer sighed. "May I have a look at Hector's file?" she asked.

"Certainly," said the Attorney General. "Ms. Walker, go get Hector's file."

She looked at him blankly.

blank lacking understanding; confused

"Well?"

The Warden turned to Mr. Pendanski. "Bring me Hector Zeroni's file."

He stared at her.

"Get it!" she ordered.

Mr. Pendanski went into the office. He returned a few minutes later and announced the file was apparently misplaced.

The Attorney General was outraged. "What kind of camp are you running here, Ms. Walker?"

The Warden said nothing. She stared at the suitcase.

The Attorney General assured Stanley's lawyer that he would get the records. "Excuse me while I call my office." He turned back to the Warden. "I assume the phone works." He walked into the camp office, slamming the door behind him. A little while later he reappeared and told the Warden he wanted to talk to her.

She cursed, then went inside.

Stanley gave Zero a thumbs-up.

"Caveman? Is that you?"

He turned to see Armpit and Squid coming out of the Wreck Room. Squid shouted back into the Wreck Room, "Caveman and Zero are out here!"

Soon all the boys from Group D had gathered around him and Zero.

"Good to see you, man," Armpit said, shaking his hand. "We thought you were buzzard food."

"Stanley is being released today," said Mr. Pendanski.

"Way to go," said Magnet, hitting him on the shoulder.

"And you didn't even have to step on a rattlesnake," said Squid.

Even Zigzag shook Stanley's hand. "Sorry about ... you know."

"Its cool," said Stanley.

"We had to lift the truck clear out of the hole," Zigzag told him. "It took everybody in C, D, and E. We just picked it right up."

"It was really cool," said Twitch.

X-Ray was the only one who didn't come over. Stanley saw him hang back behind the others a moment, then return to the Wreck Room.

"Guess what?" said Magnet, glancing at Mr. Pendanski. "Mom says we don't have to dig any more holes."

"That's great," Stanley said.

"Will you do me a favor?" asked Squid.

"I guess," Stanley agreed, somewhat hesitantly.

"I want you to –" He turned to Ms. Morengo. "Hey, lady, you have a pen and paper I can borrow?"

She gave it to him, and Squid wrote down a phone number which he gave to Stanley. "Call my mom for me, okay? Tell

to announce to state; declare
misplaced temporarily lost
★ **outraged** extremely angry and shocked

to assure to promise that sth will happen so that people feel reassured
record a written account of sth
to slam to close noisily and forcefully

★ **to curse** *fluchen*

Wreck Room name of a room indicating that the occupants are in a bad condition

★ **to do sb a favor** *jdm einen Gefallen tun*

★**to hesitate** to hold back or be slow to act
hesitation a state of doubt or uncertainty
hesitant uncertain

to depart to leave

to locate to find where sth is

to access here: to enter a computer file and get information from it

to confine to keep sb locked up

to incarcerate to imprison

her ... Tell her I said I was sorry. Tell her *Alan* said he was sorry."

Stanley promised he would.

"Now you be careful out in the real world," said Armpit. "Not everybody is as nice as us."

Stanley smiled.

The boys departed when the Warden came out of the office. The Attorney General was right behind her.

"My office is having some difficulty locating Hector Zeroni's records," the Attorney General said.

"So you have no claim of authority over him?" asked Ms. Morengo.

"I didn't say that. He's in the computer. We just can't access his records. It's like they've fallen through a hole in cyberspace."

"A hole in cyberspace," Ms. Morengo repeated. "How interesting. When is his release date?"

"I don't know."

"How long has he been here?"

"Like I said, we can't –"

"So what are you planning to do with him? Keep him confined indefinitely, without justification, while you go crawling through black holes in cyberspace?"

The Attorney General stared at her. "He was obviously incarcerated for a reason."

"Oh? And what reason was that?"

The Attorney General said nothing.

Stanley's lawyer took hold of Zero's hand. "C'mon, "Hector, you're coming with us."

49

to anchor to use an anchor *(Anker)* to hold a boat, ship, etc. in one place

There never used to be yellow-spotted lizards in the town of Green Lake. They didn't come to the area until after the lake dried up. But the townsfolk had heard about the "red-eyed monsters" living in the desert hills.

One afternoon, Sam, the onion man, and his donkey, Mary Lou, were returning to his boat, which was anchored just a little off shore. It was late in November and the peach trees had lost most of their leaves.

"Sam!" someone called.

He turned around to see three men running after him, waving their hats. He waited. "Afternoon, Walter. Bo, Jesse," he greeted them, as they walked up, catching their breath.

"Glad we caught you," said Bo. "We're going rattlesnake hunting in the morning."

"We want to get some of your lizard juice," said Walter.

"I ain't a-scared of no rattlesnake," said Jesse. "But I don't want to come across one of those red-eyed monsters. I seen one once, and that was enough. I knew about the red eyes, of course. I hadn't heard about the big black teeth."

I ain't a-scared I am not scared

"It's the white tongues that get me," said Bo.

Sam gave each man two bottles of pure onion juice. He told them to drink one bottle before going to bed that night, then a half bottle in the morning, and then a half bottle around lunchtime.

"You sure this stuff works?" asked Walter.

"I tell you what," said Sam. "If it doesn't, you can come back next week and I'll give you your money back."

Walter looked around unsure, as Bo and Jesse laughed. Then Sam laughed, too. Even Mary Lou let out a rare hee-haw.

hee-haw imitation of the braying sound a donkey makes

"Just remember," Sam told the men before they left. "It's very important you drink a bottle tonight. You got to get it into your bloodstream. The lizards don't like onion blood."

bloodstream the flow of blood through a living body

Stanley and Zero sat in the backseat of Ms. Morengo's BMW. The suitcase lay between them. It was locked, and they decided they'd let Stanley's father try to open it in his workshop.

Why did the lizards not bite or kill Stanley and Zero?

"You don't know what's in it, do you?" she asked.

"No," said Stanley.

"I didn't think so."

The air-conditioning was on, but they drove with the windows open as well, because, "No offense, but you boys really smell bad."

Ms. Morengo explained that she was a patent attorney. "I'm helping your father with the new product he's invented. He happened to mention your situation, so I did a little investigation. Clyde Livingston's sneakers were stolen sometime before 3:15. I found a young man, Derrick Dunne, who said that at 3:20 you were in the bathroom fishing your notebook out of the toilet. Two girls remembered seeing you come out of the boys' restroom carrying a wet notebook."

patent attorney an attorney who has specialized qualifications for representing clients in obtaining patents and acting in all matters relating to patent law

Stanley felt his ears redden. Even after everything he'd been through, the memory still caused him to feel shame.

"So you couldn't have stolen them," said Ms. Morengo.

★to advise to counsel
advice opinion(s) or recommendation(s) offered as a guide to action
advisable likely to produce a good outcome

to eliminate to remove or get rid of totally

★ **spicy** *würzig*

★ **familiar** well-known or easily recognizable because you have seen, heard, or experienced it before

"He didn't. I did," said Zero.

"You did what?" asked Ms. Morengo.

"I stole the sneakers."

The lawyer actually turned around while driving and looked at him. "I didn't hear that," she said. "And I advise you to make sure I don't hear it again."

"What did my father invent?" Stanley asked. "Did he find a way to recycle sneakers?"

"No, he's still working on that," explained Ms. Morengo. "But he invented a product that eliminates foot odor. Here, I've got a sample in my briefcase. I wish I had more. You two could bathe in it."

She opened her briefcase with one hand and passed a small bottle back to Stanley. It had a fresh and somewhat spicy smell. He handed it to Zero.

"What's it called?" Stanley asked.

"We haven't come up with a name yet," said Ms. Morengo.

"It smells familiar," said Zero.

"Peaches, right'" asked Ms. Morengo. "That's what everyone says."

A short while later both boys fell asleep. Behind them the sky had turned dark, and for the first time in over a hundred years, a drop of rain fell into the empty lake.

PART THREE

FILLING IN THE HOLES

50

curse a word or sentence used to ask God or a magical power to do sth bad to sb or sth; *Fluch*

desperate here: extreme, very great

★to dedicate to commit
dedication commitment
dedicated committed

to tend to be inclined
tedious tiresomely wordy and uninteresting
★ **self-confidence** pride and faith in your own abilities and strengths
subtle not noticeable straightaway
to pry open to force sth open using a lever
to gasp to suddenly draw in breath from shock or surprise

stock certificate a document issued by a company certifying ownership of one or more of its shares

deed of trust a document that transfers the legal title of a property to a trustee

promissory note a document, usually negotiable, containing a signed promise to pay a stated sum of money to a specified person at a designated date or on demand

fee payment for a service
★ **laboratory** building or room equipped for conducting scientific research or for teaching practical science

Stanley's mother insists that there never was a curse. She even doubts whether Stanley's great-great-grandfather really stole a pig. The reader might find it interesting, however, that Stanley's father invented his cure for foot odor the day after the great-great-grandson of Elya Yelnats carried the great-great-great-grandson of Madame Zeroni up the mountain.

The Attorney General closed Camp Green Lake. Ms. Walker, who was in desperate need of money, had to sell the land which had been in her family for generations. It was bought by a national organization dedicated to the well-being of young girls. In a few years, Camp Green Lake will become a Girl Scout camp.

This is pretty much the end of the story. The reader probably still has some questions, but unfortunately, from here on in, the answers tend to be long and tedious. While Mrs. Bell, Stanley's former math teacher, might want to know the percent change in Stanley's weight, the reader probably cares more about the change in Stanley's character and self-confidence. But those changes are subtle and hard to measure. There is no simple answer.

Even the contents of the suitcase turned out to be somewhat tedious, Stanley's father pried it open in his workshop, and at first everyone gasped at the sparkling jewels. Stanley thought he and Hector had become millionaires. But the jewels were of poor quality, worth no more than twenty thousand dollars.

Underneath the jewels was a stack of papers that had once belonged to the first Stanley Yelnats. These consisted of stock certificates, deeds of trust, and promissory notes. They were hard to read and even more difficult to understand. Ms. Morengo's law firm spent more than two months going through all the papers.

They turned out to be a lot more valuable than the jewels. After legal fees and taxes, Stanley and Zero each received less than a million dollars.

But not a lot less.

It was enough for Stanley to buy his family a new house, with a laboratory in the basement, and for Hector to hire a team of private investigators.

But it would be boring to go through all the tedious details of all the changes in their lives. Instead, the reader will be presented with one last scene, which took place almost a year and a half after Stanley and Hector left Camp Green Lake. You will have to fill in the holes yourself.

***

There was a small party at the Yelnats house. Except for Stanley and Hector, everyone there was an adult. All kinds of snacks and drinks were set out on the counter, including caviar, champagne, and the fixings to make ice cream sundaes.

The Super Bowl was on television, but nobody was really watching.

"It should be coming on at the next break," Ms. Morengo announced.

A time-out was called in the football game, and a commercial on the screen.

Everyone stopped talking and watched.

The commercial showed a baseball game. Amid a cloud of dust, Clyde Livingston slid into home plate as the catcher caught the ball and tried to tag him out.

"Safe!" shouted the umpire as he signaled with his arms.

The people at Stanley's house cheered, as if the run really counted.

Clyde Livingston got up and dusted the dirt off his uniform. As he made his way back to the dugout he spoke to the camera. "Hi, I'm Clyde Livingston, but everyone around here calls me 'Sweet Feet.'"

"Way to go, Sweet Feet!" said another baseball player, slapping his hand.

Besides being on the television screen, Clyde Livingston was also sitting on the couch next to Stanley.

"But my feet weren't always sweet," the television Clyde Livingston said as he sat down on the dugout bench. "They used to smell so bad that nobody would sit near me in the dugout."

"They really did stink," said the woman sitting on the couch on the other side of Clyde. She held her nose with one hand, and fanned air with the other.

Clyde shushed her.

"Then a teammate told me about Sploosh," said the television Clyde. He pulled a can of Sploosh out from under the dugout bench and held it up for everyone to see. "I just spray

the fixings here: the ingredients

Super Bowl the main championship game of the sport of American Rules Football, held annually in January between the champions of the American Football Conference and the National Football Conference

commercial an advertisement on radio or television
home plate in baseball: the base that a pitcher must throw the ball over for a strike and that a player must safely reach in order to score a run; *Schlagmal*
catcher in baseball: *Fänger*
to tag out in baseball: to touch a base runner with the ball while that player is in between bases, thereby getting them out
umpire *Schiedsrichter*

dugout in baseball: the place where the rest of the batting team sits while they are waiting to bat

to fan to create a current of air by moving your hand back and forth
to shush to make the "sh" sound to silence sb

tingle a prickling sensation

★ **ingredient** component, element
fungus *Pilz*

a little on each foot every morning, and now I really do have sweet feet. Plus, I like the tingle."

"Splоosh," said a voice. "A treat for your feet. Made from all natural ingredients, it neutralizes odor-causing fungi and bacteria. Plus, you'll like the tingle."

Everyone at the party clapped their hands.

"He wasn't lying," said the woman who sat next to Clyde. "I couldn't even be in the same room with his socks."

The other people at the party laughed.

The woman continued. "I'm not joking. It was so bad –"

"You've made your point," said Clyde, covering her mouth with his hand. He looked back at Stanley. "Will you do me a favor, Stanley?"

Stanley raised and lowered his left shoulder.

"I'm going to get more caviar," said Clyde. "Keep your hand over my wife's mouth." He patted Stanley on the shoulder as he rose from the couch.

Stanley looked uncertainly at his hand, then at Clyde Livingston's wife.

to wink to quickly close and open one eye

She winked at him.

He felt himself blush, and turned away toward Hector, who was sitting on the floor in front of an overstuffed chair.

absent-minded without concentrating
to fluff to make sth look fuller and puffier
weathered *wettergegerbt*

A woman sitting in the chair behind Hector was absent-mindedly fluffing his hair with her fingers. She wasn't very old, but her skin had a weathered look to it, almost like leather. Her eyes seemed weary, as if she'd seen too many things in her life that she didn't want to see. And when she smiled, her mouth seemed too big for her face.

Very softly, she half sang, half hummed a song that her grandmother used to sing to her when she was a little girl.

If only, if only, the moon speaks no reply;
Reflecting the sun and all that's gone by.
Be strong, my weary wolf turn around boldly.
Fly high, my baby bird,
My angel, my only.

★**bold** courageous
boldness courage

Con-Texts and additional material

About the author

Louis Sachar was born in New York on March 20, 1954, but moved with his family to Tustin, California when he was nine years old. In high school, he became an avid reader, and later started college in Ohio. During his first semester, however, his father died, so he moved back to California to be near his mother. There, he majored in Economics at Berkeley, and also took a class working as a teacher's aide at an elementary school. After graduating in 1976, he decided to write a children's book at night while working at a sweater warehouse during the day, but ended up being fired. He then chose to go to law school in San Francisco, graduating in 1980 and working as a lawyer till 1989, when he gave up his legal career to write children's books full time instead. He married in 1985 and had a daughter in 1987. Today, he lives in Austin, Texas with his family.

His most famous book is *Holes*, which won the National Book Award in 1998, but he has also written books about the fictional Wayside School *(Sideways Stories from Wayside School)*, the *Marvin Redpost* children's book series and various other books. There are two sequels to *Holes*: *Stanley Yelnats' Survival Guide to Camp Green Lake (2003) and Small Steps (2006)*.

A day in the life of a teenager in boot camp

The decision to send your teenage son or daughter to a juvenile boot camp is not an easy one to make. A boot camp for teenagers is not like sending a child to Boy Scout camp or to a church youth group retreat. The objective of a juvenile boot camp is to dramatically and radically change the behavior, the thinking patterns and the priorities of troubled youth who are in their care. That means that the experiences your teenager will have at a boot camp setting will be difficult, challenging and unrelenting.

unrelenting *gnadenlos, unerbittlich*

A typical day in the life of a teenager who is at a juvenile boot camp will not be like anything he or she has ever experienced before. There will be a routine to it that will quickly become familiar. Variety will not be a big part of what your teenager does each day. The use of repetitive tasks and a reliable schedule is part of the reorientation of the kids who come to a boot camp for teenagers. But that routine daily schedule will be far from easy.

repetitive doing the same thing many times

The stress and effort of each day will tire your son or daughter out in ways they never considered possible. But because each day will be one of regular, short term tasks that are difficult to do, that lifestyle will reorient the way a troubled youth thinks and views life. Those short term tasks will provide short term gratification when a teenager completes them correctly. In many ways, just not being in trouble with the drill sergeant for one day will be reward enough. The drill sergeants will be demanding, loud, unforgiving and harsh.

to reorient sth *etw neu ausrichten*

[...]

No saying no

During any given day during your son or daughter's stay at a juvenile boot camp, there will be tremendous pressure and demands put on them to perform up to the standards of the drill instructor. Unlike how authority your teenager may have encountered before his or her boot camp experience, there is no saying "no" to a boot camp instructor. The demand put on the teenagers in camp are not a request. Com-

to encounter to experience

request question, polite demand

pliance is not only assumed, it is enforced and disobedience is treated harshly with hard labor or a prison like experience.

compliance the practice of obeying rules; obedience

What happens each day

A day in the life of a teenager at a juvenile boot camp begins early and the pace is nonstop all day long. Even before breakfast, there is often a time of calisthenics or even more difficult exercise. In some juvenile boot camps, a five mile run before breakfast is not uncommon. The one thing that is consistent of almost any youth who goes to a boot camp for teenagers is he or she will come back from the camp experience in good shape.

calisthenics physical exercises intended to develop a strong body

Meals are ample and usually well prepared at a juvenile boot camp. The level of activity is so demanding on the kids in a boot camp for teenagers that they will need a lot of good nutrition and high protein fuel to keep their bodies going. While the youth in a boot camp experience may have a lot to complain about, the quality or quantity of food is rarely the problem.

ample large, enough

nutrition *Ernährung*
protein *Eiweiß*

The typical day in a juvenile boot camp is busy with exercise and other physical challenges. Many of those challenges will call upon the teenagers in the camp to work together or they cannot make it through what they must do. Learning to work together creates a bond between the youth who are forged into a unit that can function together quite well by the end of the boot camp experience.

bond connection

[...]

When your teenager returns from a juvenile boot camp, you will be living with a youth who knows what a regimented lifestyle of hard work is all about. His or her attitudes toward relationships, goals and priorities will be changed forever. The lifestyle at boot camp will alter those values for the better and permanently as well. So while it is a tough decision to put a troubled youth in a juvenile boot camp, in many cases it will bring about a change for the better that could not have been achieved any other way.

regimented controlled strictly

to alter to change

to achieve to get as the result of action; to gain

from Troubled Teen Boot Camps, http://www.teenbootcamps.org/boot-camps/a-day-in-the-life-of-a-teenager-in-boot-camp.html, 2015 [04.02.2015]

Michael Janofsky: States pressed as 3 boys die at boot camps

substantially very much

to assert to state clearly
severity *Ernst, Schwere*

to enroll to arrange that sb can officially join a group, course, etc.

to compel to cause, force, demand

disparity difference

The death of Tony Haynes, a 14-year-old, in the Arizona desert this month is increasing calls for stronger regulation of outdoor camps for troubled youths, an industry that has grown substantially over the last 20 years.

At least 31 teenagers in 11 states have died at these camps since 1980, including 3 this year, in widely diverse circumstances.

In Arizona, investigators said they were told that before Tony Haynes died counselors physically abused him and forced him to eat dirt.

In February, Ryan Lewis, a 14-year-old, hanged himself at a wilderness therapy camp in West Virginia. His parents have asserted that the camp operators did not recognize the severity of his depression.

That same month in Florida, Michael Wiltsie, 12, died at a camp for troubled boys after a 320-pound counselor restrained him on the ground for nearly 30 minutes.

These are exceptional cases, given the thousands of children each year who attend such camps, normally without incident. Parents who enroll their children and teachers often credit the camps with taking young people away from gangs, drugs and alcohol and instilling in them a new maturity and sense of self-confidence. They operate on the theory that rugged conditions and tough discipline can break antisocial behavior or even criminal habits. State and local courts also use the programs, as an alternative to jail.

Yet the deaths and reports of abuses are putting increased pressure on states to adopt regulations to govern the roughly 400 boot camps operating around the country. While most states have laws against child abuse and endangerment, many do not specifically compel these camps to meet certain standards for procedures and personnel.

"There are significant disparities from state to state," said Kimball DeLaMare, a camp owner in Utah and the chairman of the National Association of Therapeutic Schools and Programs, a trade group. "Over all, they have not done too much, which is one of the reasons we are trying to develop our own standards."

Arizona is among those states that have done the least. "You have to provide more documents to get a fishing license than to run a camp for young boys," said Chris Cummiskey, a Democratic state senator. "We require nothing to demonstrate you have the qualifications to engage in this type of activity."

Industry officials say they welcome additional governmental scrutiny of the camps, some of which operate on contracts with state prison systems. "Every state that allows wilderness programs needs to have regulations in place," said Mark Lawrence, an owner of a camp in South Carolina and the chairman of the National Association of Therapeutic Wilderness Camps, another trade group. "And somebody has to monitor them."

scrutiny careful and close examination

to monitor to check

Children's advocates and parents of children who have died under supervision of camp personnel say abuses would end altogether if states got tougher, requiring camp operators to have suitable backgrounds in education, psychology or social work. "This is one of the big gaps and a big part of the problem," said Mark I. Soler, president of the Youth Law Center in Washington, a public interest law firm. "As a result, kids are not protected, and they don't even understand that they have rights. They believe the abusive treatment they get is routine."

Critics also argue that camps should have medical personnel on site, which was not the case when Tony Haynes fell unconscious in the desert. After camp counselors called 911, the boy was driven to a hospital, where he died.

Jim Crow laws

After the American Civil War (1861–1865), most southern states and, later, border states passed laws that denied blacks basic human rights. It is not clear how, but the minstrel character's name "Jim Crow" became a kind of shorthand for the laws, customs and etiquette that segregated and demeaned African Americans primarily from the 1870s to the 1960s. [...]

shorthand *Abkürzung*
to demean to make people have less respect for a person

During the Jim Crow period there were separate hospitals for blacks and whites, separate prisons, separate public and private schools, separate churches, separate cemeteries, separate

public restrooms, and separate public accommodations. In most instances, the black facilities were grossly inferior, older, smaller, less-well-kept, and less conveniently located. In other cases, there were no black facilities, no Colored public restroom, no public beach, and no place to sit or eat.
→ List of Jim Crow laws: http://www.ferris.edu/htmls/news/jimcrow/origins.htm

Intermarriage:

descent *Abstammung*

All marriages between a white person and a negro, or between a white person and a person of negro descent to the fourth generation inclusive, are hereby forever prohibited.
Florida

Cohabitation:

cohabitation Zusammenleben, eheähnliche Gemeinschaft

Any negro man and white woman, or any white man and negro woman, who are not married to each other, who shall habitually live in and occupy in the nighttime the same room shall each be punished by imprisonment not exceeding twelve (12) months, or by fine not exceeding five hundred ($500.00) dollars.
Florida

Education:

The schools for white children and the schools for negro children shall be conducted separately.
Florida
[...]

Promotion of equality:

misdemeanor bad or improper act

Any person ... who shall be guilty of printing, publishing or circulating printed, typewritten or written matter urging or presenting for public acceptance or general information, arguments or suggestions in favor of social equality or of intermarriage between whites and negroes, shall be guilty of a misdemeanor and subject to fine not exceeding five hundred ($ 500.00) dollars or imprisonment not exceeding six (6) months or both.
Mississippi

from Ferris State University: Jim Crow Museum, http://www.ferris.edu/htmls/news/jimcrow/origins.htm and http://www.ferris.edu/htmls/news/jimcrow/origins/images/jimcrowlaws.pdf, 2012 [21.10.2014]

Literary terms: Stylistic devices

allusion	A direct or indirect reference to some well-known historical person or event, saying, proverb or a line or sentence from a work of literature. An allusion often serves the purpose of revealing the writer's background and education level.
cliché	a commonplace, over-used expression, which retains little or none of its original meaning
humour	the quality of being entertaining or amusing
irony	Verbal irony is the use of words to express the opposite of their literal meaning. The writer or speaker says something he or she does not actually mean. The reader or audience understands the irony through the tone in which the words are expressed or through shared cultural values.
metaphor	two seemingly unlike things are linked with one another in the form of an implicit comparison
personification	the technique of representing animals, plants, objects, or abstract ideas as if they were a human being and possessed human qualities
pun	a figure of speech involving a play on words, in which one word has two different meanings, so that a sentence can be understood in two different ways
repetition	the repeated use of particular sounds, syllables, words, phrases, sentences, etc. in order to structure a text and achieve a particular effect

simile an element of imagery, in which distinctly different things are linked together in the form of an explicit comparison through the words "like" or "as"

symbol an element of imagery, in which a concrete object stands not only for itself, but for some abstract idea as well

The novel: Key words

atmosphere mood created by the author influenced by the setting, use of language and characterization

characters people in a fictional text presented through their actions, speech and thoughts, as well as through direct description

conflict a struggle or opposition between different forces which produces tension

flashback description of a past scene that has relevance to the plot in the present

foreshadowing anticipation, hinting at later events

mode of presentation
a) **scenic presentation:** scenes are described in great detail (including dialogue and the depiction of emotions and thoughts)
b) **panoramic presentation:** several events are summarized

narrator the voice telling the story, who is created by the author and is therefore part of the fictional world

plot the structure of events in a fictional story, which develops in a number of stages:

- **exposition:** characters, setting, theme are introduced
- **rising action:** conflict is developed
- **climax:** highest point of tension/conflict
- **turning point:** change in the conflict or suspense
- **falling action:** suspense is reduced

- **denouement:** some resolution is achieved
- **ending:** can be an open or surprise ending

point of view the perspective from which characters and events are presented

register the words, phrases and even syntactical structures that particular groups of people prefer to use and that typically identify them as members of the group in question

setting the time and place of action

style refers to the way in which something is done or presented and usually includes the attitudes of the people involved

telling name in a narrative text, this describes a person's name which reveals one or more of his or her characteristic traits

theme main topic, central subject

Characterization

How to write a characterization

1. Mark / collect all of the information that is given about a character.
2. Introduce the character and the situation he / she is in. Refer to his / her social background / position / job / role in the family.
3. Start characterizing her / him directly, i.e. give his / her age / describe outward appearance / consider what is said directly about the person (stage directions).
4. Refer to the traits of character that are revealed indirectly. Consider what a character does, how he / she reacts or behaves, what people think and feel about him / her, the mood the character is generally in, how he / she responds to others.
5. Try to sum up whether a character develops / changes in the course of events (complex / round character) or if he / she does not change his / her attitude and beliefs (flat character).

Characterization: Useful words and phrases

- [Character name] is a teenager, who is not older than 20.
- He/she … is presented/described as …
- It is said that he/she looks/seems to be …
- On the one hand, he/she is portrayed/depicted as a person who …
- On the other hand, he/she …
- It is characteristic of/typical of him/her that …
- He/she is also characterized by his/her attitude towards …/ reaction to …, which is revealed/emphasized by his/her words/reactions/gestures/facial expressions …
- He/she behaves arrogantly/pretends to be superior when …
- He/she speaks in a low/loud voice/shouts at …
- He/she shows emotions/feelings/that show that he/she is moved/nervous/excited/irritated …
- He/she seems to feel insecure/be convinced of himself/ herself/be in a bad/good mood when he/she refers to/ answers …
- This idea is revealed when he/she says that, "…" (p. …, l. …)
- He/she is aware of the fact that …
- His/her behaviour shows that he/she is curious/jealous/ frightened/taken by surprise/self-confident/convinced that …/interested in …
- His/her way of treating others is … harsh/friendly/gentle/ arrogant/patronizing/contemptuous …
- He/she creates the impression that he/she is a man/woman who …
- An essential component of his/her character is …
- The reader/audience may conclude from his/her behaviour that …
- During the novel/story/the course of action, he/she undergoes a development/remains essentially unchanged.
- He/she is a flat/complex (round) character/an individual and not just a mere stereotype.
- One can easily identify with …/we feel pity/sympathize with/ dislike him/her because …
- In conclusion, it can be said that …

Point of view

Definitions

Whenever an author tells a story, there must be a storyteller. The storyteller is not identical with the author; instead, the author chooses a narrator, who can tell the story from different angles, i. e. points of view. In the following section, the three most essential points of view are explained:

- **First-person narrator (limited narrator/point of view)**
  The first-person narrator is a character inside the story. He/she can only inform about what he/she knows, feels, thinks and experiences. The narrator can be either a main character or a minor character. Because of the narrator's direct reporting of anything that happens, the reader feels as close to the protagonist(s) as the narrator does. It is therefore easy for the reader to identify with the narrator.

- **Third-person narrator (selective-omniscient narrator/ point of view)**
  The selective-omniscient third-person narrator presents things as they are seen through the eyes of one or several characters in the story and chooses to describe the thoughts and emotions of that or those characters. The reader does not feel as close to the protagonist(s) because the narrator tells the story in the third person. He or she can therefore only identify with those characters to whose consciousness the perspective is limited.

- **Third-person narrator (omniscient narrator/point of view)**
  Omniscient narrators can move freely in time and space, shifting from character to character and reporting what they choose of each character's speech, actions, thoughts, feelings and emotions. They may give additional comments or simply decide to show the action without judgment. As the term "omniscient" suggests, this perspective enables the narrator to "know everything" and to enter the minds of all of the characters. This means that the reader can easily identify with them. Nevertheless, he or she does not feel spoken to directly as, for instance, when a first-person narrator tells a story.

Point of view: Useful phrases

- The story is told from the point of view of …
- The author uses a (first-person) narrator.
- The narrator reports what he or she observes/relates the events in an objective/subjective way.
- to be crucial to the reader's understanding of the story
- to make a deeper impact/impression on the reader